All-Time Favorite

RELIEF CARVING Projects

The Best of
WOODCARVING
ILLUSTRATED

Expert Instruction & Techniques from *Woodcarving Illustrated*

FOX CHAPEL
PUBLISHING

ISBN 978-1-4971-0537-9

Library of Congress Control Number: 2025900053

To learn more about the other great books from Fox Chapel Publishing, or to find a retailer near you, call toll-free at 800-457-9112 or visit us at www.FoxChapelPublishing.com.
You can also send mail to:
Fox Chapel Publishing
903 Square Street
Mount Joy, PA 17552

We are always looking for talented authors.
To submit an idea, please send a brief inquiry to acquisitions@foxchapelpublishing.com.

Printed in China
First printing

Because working with wood and woodworking tools inherently includes the risk of injury and damage, this book cannot guarantee that creating the projects in this book is safe for everyone. For this reason, this book is sold without warranties or guarantees of any kind, expressed or implied, and the publisher and the author disclaim any liability for any injuries, losses, or damages caused in any way by the content of this book or the reader's use of the tools needed to complete the projects presented here. The publisher and the author urge all readers to thoroughly review each project and to understand the use of all tools before beginning any project.

Introduction

Relief carving is a distinct and sophisticated form of woodworking that requires precision, insight into material properties, and an understanding of complex techniques. *All-Time Favorite Relief Carving Projects* is designed to demystify the process of relief carving, providing woodworkers of all skill levels with the necessary tools and knowledge to excel in this craft.

This book begins with a thorough examination of the tools essential for relief carving, detailing their specific uses and handling to maximize their effectiveness. We delve into the variety of woods most suitable for relief projects, discussing their characteristics and how they influence the carving process.

Key techniques are the cornerstone of this guide. You'll learn critical skills, such as the execution of undercuts and stop cuts, how to approach building layers in your carving, and a variety of finishing techniques—to name just a few. These methods are vital for achieving the depth and detail that relief carving is known for.

Additionally, the book addresses the efficient use of resources in the workshop. By focusing on projects that vary in complexity, carvers can gradually build their skill set without significant waste of materials or time. This approach ensures that each project not only enhances your proficiency but also contributes to a broader understanding of woodworking.

Whether you're looking to refine your technique or start a new journey in woodworking, this book provides the guidance and expertise necessary to undertake any relief carving project with confidence.

14

28

84

Table of Contents

90

98

46

72

104

116

Getting Started

Before you dive into the intricate world of relief carving, it's important to set a solid foundation. This chapter will introduce you to the essential tools and materials you'll need, from selecting the right kind of wood to choosing the best carving tools for different textures and effects. We'll also cover setting up your carving space to optimize safety and comfort, ensuring that you can focus on enjoying the creative process. Whether you're setting up a small corner of your home for carving or have access to a full workshop, these guidelines will help you begin your carving journey on the right foot.

Relief Carving Woods

Experienced carvers will tell you to find a source for properly seasoned wood with solid carving capability. It may require a short drive to a lumberyard, or a package delivery from a hardwood seller across the country, but getting good carving stock is paramount to your future as a carver.

The following woods will provide you with many hours of pleasurable carving, present surmountable challenges, and yield beautiful finished carvings.

Eastern White Pine

A great choice for new carvers, pine carves with little effort compared to most hardwoods. Pine has straight and even grain, and is lightweight, inexpensive, and easy to find, making it a contender for your go-to practice blanks. You can use almost any blade on pine, but make sure your tools are sharp, as pine will frequently chip out when cut with a dull blade. It glues, sands, and paints well, but resists staining because of its resins.

Eastern White Pine, Janka value: 380

Basswood

Check the Materials & Tools listings in any project in *WCI* and, more likely than not, this is the wood used. Classified as a hardwood, it is easy to carve. The grain is straight with few blemishes and holds fine details. It carves well with or across the grain. Basswood sands nicely and accepts glues, stains, and paints. A favorite wood for relief, caricature, and chip carving, it carves cleanly with edged tools.

Basswood, Janka value: 410

Butternut

Referred to as "white walnut," this hardwood is fairly easy to carve. The grain is straight yet distinctive. It carves well with the grain, resulting in a polished look. Cross-grain cutting requires extremely sharp tools to prevent splitting. Butternut is used for carving in the round, relief, and chip carving. The true beauty of the wood becomes apparent when the carving is finished with oil.

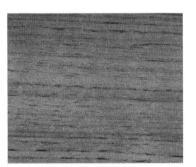

Butternut, Janka value: 490

Mahogany

Considered an exotic hardwood, mahogany is a carving staple. Maintaining sharp edges on your tools lets you cut mahogany without heavy effort. It carves well with the grain but may want to split in crosscuts. It

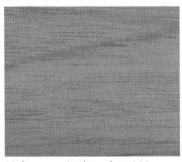

Mahogany, Janka value: 800

holds detail well, and small files and rasps will help you shape in tight places where carving tools may break the wood. It works with palm and long-handled tools as well as power carving burrs.

Water Tupelo

Tupelo is prized by wildfowl and fish carvers. The wood is super lightweight and floats perfectly for duck decoys. Because of its fine texture and interlocked grain, it power carves beautifully with virtually no fuzz-up. It holds fine details, woodburns nicely, and paints exceptionally well. Tupelo will carve cleanly with a knife but can be a challenge with other edged tools.

Water Tupelo, Janka value: 870

Cherry

Long valued for cabinetry, cherry has found favor in carving circles, as well. Its heartwood is preferred and ranges from pink to red in color. The grain is even, tight, and lightly figured, and holds detail well. When the wood is green, it carves more easily. When fully dry, cherry can become too hard to whittle, but it is ideal for relief and power carving. Cherry is also a perfect wood for making spoons and cutting boards.

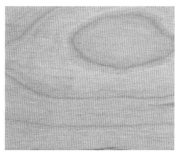

Cherry, Janka value: 950

Walnut

The appeal of this wood lies in its rich brown color and subtle grain figuration. The hardest wood in this listing, walnut can be carved with hand and rotary tools. You can get finer details with gouges and palm tools. It may require more deliberate effort and sharp tools, but carvers agree that it's worth it. Walnut works for all types of carving and appears incredibly rich when finished with oil.

Walnut, Janka value: 1010

Relief Carving Tools

Essential Gouges

While there are nearly more specialty tools and gouges than one could name, there are a handful that any aspiring relief carver should have in their arsenal. Along with your standard carving knives, the gouges listed here will equip you to make any of the projects in this book. In a later section, we will discuss specialty tools that may help make your carving experience even more enjoyable (page 8.)

Straight Gouge

The straight gouge is a fundamental tool in any woodcarver's kit, characterized by its flat, uncurved cutting edge and cylindrical profile. This tool is indispensable for making smooth, flat cuts across the grain or along the wood's surface. Its straightforward design makes it perfect for quickly removing wood and smoothing out areas, allowing for precision and control in both rough shaping and finer finishing tasks. Ideal for beginners and experts alike, the straight gouge is a versatile implement suited for a variety of carving projects.

U-Gouge

The U-gouge is another fundamental tool in the repertoire of any woodcarver, distinguished by its U-shaped curved cutting edge that is indispensable for scooping out large areas of wood. This tool is ideal for creating deep, smooth hollows and rounded channels in wood, facilitating rapid material removal while maintaining a clean surface. U-gouges come in various sizes, each designated by the width of the cutting edge and the sweep of the curve, allowing for a range of applications from roughing out to more detailed and refined carving. Their ability to carve wide, yet precise, grooves makes them especially valuable in shaping and defining the contours of both artistic sculptures and functional woodwork.

V-Tool

The V-tool, often called a parting tool, is distinguished by its V-shaped cutting edge that makes it ideal for creating sharp, clean lines and adding fine details to your work. This tool excels in carving crisp, linear details,

such as veins in leaves or decorative outlines. Its angled sides allow for precise cuts that create distinct textures and patterns. When using the V-tool, it's best to apply consistent pressure and work along the grain to prevent the wood from splitting, thereby achieving smooth and consistent grooves that enhance the overall visual appeal of the carving.

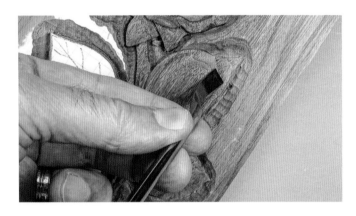

Spoon Gouge

This tool's spoon-shaped design allows you to carve concave areas where traditional straight gouges won't fit. The gouge's design gives you less resistance, allowing you to glide easily through cuts. Since you are scooping into the wood, it's better to make small, shallow cuts, slicing your way down to the depth, than making one aggressive cut.

Back-Bent Gouge

The back-bent gouge looks similar to the spoon gouge, except the cutting edge is reversed (convex instead of concave). This tool is excellent at removing wood on the underside of your piece. For example, when using

it on the leaves, you can create deep undercuts, creating shadows and depth.

Fishtail Gouge

This specialized woodcarving tool characterized by its flared, fishtail-shaped end, which allows for precision and accessibility in tight spaces. Its unique design is ideal for detailed work in corners and intricate patterns, offering a mix of fine detailing and the ability to remove larger amounts of wood. This gouge is essential for carvers who need precision and control in their projects, making it a valuable addition to any woodcarving toolkit.

Specialty Tools

You may need more precise tools to tackle more intricate projects. You can source relief carving tools from a range of specialty woodcarving tool manufacturers. Here are a few you may not have tried:

Skew Chisel

This is such a versatile tool. An angled blade makes it easy to cut with and against the grain. The size of this $5/16$" (8mm) palm skew chisel will allow you to get into tight areas, such as between the leaves.

Dental Pick

This is a great tool to reach into all the nooks and crannies of your carving.

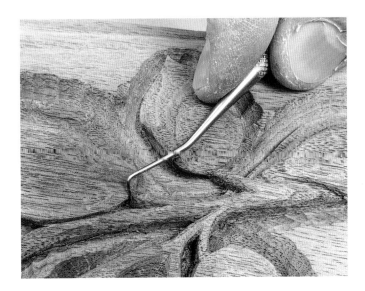

Skewed Spoon Gouge

Like the name suggests, it's a skew chisel with a spoon's shape. A fantastic tool for reaching deep into your carving to clean up those hard-to-reach angled corners with ease. If your budget allows it, purchase these tools as a mirrored pair.

Dogleg Skew Chisel

This 90-degree bent skew chisel is perfect for leveling out the background of your relief carving or to reach into deep nooks and crannies.

Bent V-Parting Tool

This is like the traditional V-parting tool, except it has a spoon shape bent toward the cutting edge. This allows you to get into areas of the carving that a straight V-parting tool would not be able to reach.

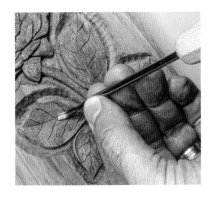

Micro Gouges

Micro gouges are designed for precision and detail in woodcarving, particularly useful in miniature and intricate projects.

Characterized by their very small, finely shaped cutting edges, these gouges allow carvers to achieve extremely detailed and delicate work that larger gouges cannot handle. Micro gouges come in a variety of shapes including U-shaped, V-shaped, and spoon-shaped, each tailored for specific types of cuts, from tight curves and corners to fine lines and texturing. Their small size and precise cutting capability make them indispensable for adding subtle details and textures to smaller carvings, enhancing the overall intricacy and finesse of the artwork.

Tip: Keeping Gouges Sharp

Using a strop regularly helps maintain the edge of your gouges, minimizing the need for more abrasive sharpening methods like stones.

1. **Clean the Gouge:** Remove any debris or residue from the blade using a cloth.
2. **Prepare the Strop:** Apply honing compound to the leather strop to enhance the sharpening process.
3. **Stropping the Gouge:** Hold the gouge at a consistent angle (typically 20-25 degrees). Use a smooth, sweeping motion to slide the cutting edge across the strop, being careful to cover the entire curvature of the edge. Repeat this process 10-15 times on each side of the gouge.
4. **Check for Burrs:** Feel for any small burrs on the back edge of the gouge and lightly strop the back side, if necessary.
5. **Test the Sharpness:** Test the gouge on a piece of scrap wood to ensure it cuts cleanly and effortlessly.

Relief Carving Tips and Techniques

If you're just getting started in relief carving, there's a lot to take in. This section discusses making your own relief carving panels, pattern transfer, finding carving depth, and sanding and finishing. As you pick up new tricks and techniques, be sure to incorporate them into your toolkit and carry them with you throughout your carving journey.

Making Your Own Relief Panels

Learning how to make your own relief panels is an important technique to counteract the tendency of flat panels to warp and cup as you carve (see **Figure 1**). This simple, straightforward, and time-tested "camber method" lets you construct panels that are stable and attractive, allowing you to focus on your carving.

To build camber (or convexity) into relief panels, you'll laminate a number of wood pieces together. The following steps and illustrations explain how this method works. To make your own panels using this method, you'll need a saw capable of cutting and ripping boards, a planer, a jointer, yellow carpenter's glue, pipe clamps, and C-clamps.

Step 1. Cut the pieces to length and rip them to widths of 3"–4" (7.6–10.2cm). Plane them to a uniform thickness.

Step 2. Mark the surface of each board that will appear on the carved side of the panel. If possible, you'll want to choose the sapwood side of the board because it will have growth rings with a larger arc. Use the heartwood side for the back of the panel because those growth rings have a smaller arc. The sapwood also tends to be lighter than the heartwood, and the lighter sapwood enhances the appearance of the finished carving.

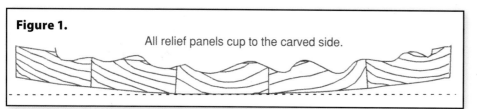

Figure 1.

All relief panels cup to the carved side.

Flat relief panels cup after carving, as shown, unless slight bow is designed into the carving panel.

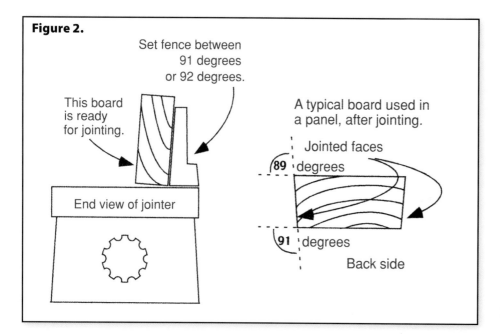

Figure 2.

Set fence between 91 degrees or 92 degrees.

This board is ready for jointing.

End view of jointer

A typical board used in a panel, after jointing.

Jointed faces

89 degrees

91 degrees

Back side

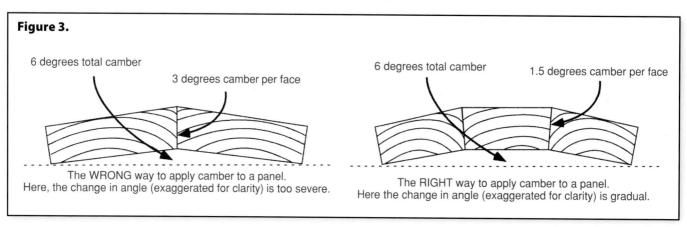

Figure 3.

6 degrees total camber

3 degrees camber per face

The WRONG way to apply camber to a panel.
Here, the change in angle (exaggerated for clarity) is too severe.

6 degrees total camber

1.5 degrees camber per face

The RIGHT way to apply camber to a panel.
Here the change in angle (exaggerated for clarity) is gradual.

Step 3. Arrange the boards as they will appear in the finished relief panel, and get the jointer ready. Set the jointer fence to either 91 or 92 degrees, deviating one or two degrees from the typical 90 degrees (see **Figure 2**). This way, when the boards are joined edge to edge, they will form a curvature similar to that of a wooden barrel (see **Figure 3**).

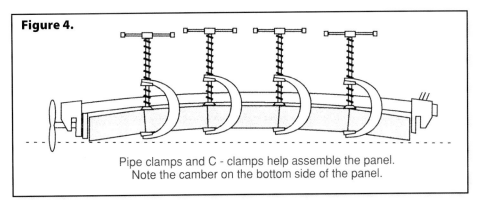

Figure 4.

Pipe clamps and C - clamps help assemble the panel.
Note the camber on the bottom side of the panel.

Step 4. Glue the boards together with yellow carpenter's glue. Place pipe clamps across the boards and C-clamps at each joint to prevent the boards from moving out of position (see **Figure 4**). After the pipe clamps are tightened, the C-clamps can be removed.

Step 5. The result is a panel that is convex on the side to be carved (see **Figure 5**). During the carving process, the panel cups towards the carved side as predicted, using up most of the camber built into the panel. However, some camber should remain. If the finished carving is hung on the wall, the remaining camber will not be visible, but it actually aids in the hanging of the carving.

Pattern Transfer

When it comes to transferring the pattern to the wood, we recommend one of three techniques:

1. Using a craft glue stick, apply the pattern directly to the wood. With this technique, you need to sand off the excess paper and glue before applying the finish.

2. Place a sheet of graphite transfer paper between the wood and the pattern, using blue painter's tape to hold into place. Then, using a stylus tool or ballpoint pen (a pencil may tear the pattern), trace the pattern, transferring the image onto the wood.

3. Use a pounce wheel tool to carefully trace over the pattern. This tool will leave tiny indentations in the wood. Then, using a pencil, connect these tiny indentations to reveal the blueprint image.

Figure 5. When relief panel boards are glued up, a slight bow should result. Carving the covex side causes the panel to flatten out.

Tip: Ebony and Ivory

Graphite transfer paper comes in black and white. Use white to transfer images to darker woods, so you can easily see the image.

Measuring Depth

When carving deep-relief projects, it's important to know how deep you are carving into the project because wood expands and contracts based on temperature and humidity changes. If you remove too much wood from the background, your project can cup or warp, creating small cracks in the delicate portions of your carving. To minimize this process, leave more wood than you take away, and don't carve lower than half the thickness of the wood. To help stick to these guidelines, measure the depth as you carve by making a depth gauge from paper stock and making two marks on your gauge. One marks the thickness of the wood (in this case, it's ¾" [19mm]), and the other marks a little over half that height (⅜" [10mm]). Then, shade the upper portion red. Next, from the back of the plaque, slide the gauge into the saw

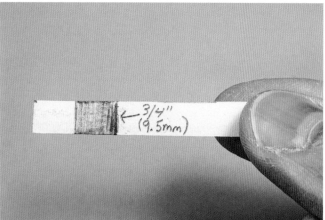

Use a depth gauge (you can make one out of cardstock) to check your carving depth as you go.

kerf with the ¾" (19mm) mark flush with the plaque. Then, view the gauge from the front of the plaque; if you don't see red, you didn't go past the halfway mark.

Sanding

To sand your finished carving, place a sheet of 120-grit sandpaper on a flat surface and, while holding the plaque on its edges, carefully sand the entire front and back of the plaque, going in the direction of the grain. Depending on the pattern transfer technique you used, repeat this process (and vacuum the sawdust from the project frequently) until you remove all the residual pattern, glue, and/or pencil markings. Move to 150-grit sandpaper and repeat. During this process, you might unintentionally sand some of your carving. Look it over and fine-tune those areas.

Applying a Finish

Apply all finishes in a well-ventilated area, wearing disposable rubber gloves and eyewear. Always practice on scrap wood first to make sure you like the look. Also be sure to dispose of your rags and brushes carefully; finishes may generate heat as they cure or when reacting to oxygen in the air and can spontaneously combust. Here are a few that work well:

Wipe-On Polyurethane: Using a disposable paintbrush, apply a liberal amount of wipe-on polyurethane (satin or gloss, depending on your preference), and immediately wipe it off using a cotton rag. Use an additional disposable brush and/or rag to remove any excess puddling in the nooks and crannies. Allow the finish to dry, following the manufacturer's instructions. Using very fine steel wool (grade #0000), carefully buff the finish and remove (with a vacuum or soft brush) any steel wool debris. Apply a second coat of wipe-on polyurethane using the technique previously described.

Boiled Linseed Oil and Howard Feed-N-Wax: Apply a liberal amount of boiled linseed oil over the entire carving using a disposable brush. Let it soak into the carving for about seven minutes, and remove the excess by rubbing with a clean rag. Allow the finish to dry for at least three days. Next, apply Howard® Feed-N-Wax with a disposable brush. Let it set for at least 20 minutes, and then rub off the excess. Buff using a shoe brush, and set aside to dry for two days.

Beginner Projects

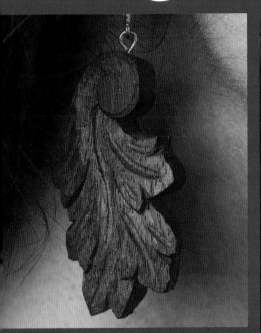

Bark Fairy Door

BY ADRIA LAYCRAFT

I love to have whimsical decorations around my garden and home, so carving fairy doors out of bark seemed like an obvious project. Cottonwood bark lends itself to the rustic nature of the cottage-style door. The techniques used to create the door are the same ones to make stone and wooden boards on fairy houses, so the techniques are transferable to bigger projects. Carving just the door instead of a whole house is a great beginner project with quick, gratifying results. Thanks to the never-ending variety of bark shapes, no two doors will look exactly alike!

To carve a sturdy fairy door in bark, use a small handsaw or power saw of your choice to take off the end of a long piece of carving bark. Cottonwood and balsam poplar bark work well. Use the end of a long hunk of bark that's dry and free of bug holes. The flat end you create will be the base of the door. Scrape the front clean of raw outer bark to reveal the orangey layer underneath. Leave the raw bark on the sides.

Tools and Materials
- Cottonwood or balsam poplar bark, 1" to 2" (2.5 to 5.1cm) thick; approx. 3" x 5" (7.6cm x 12.7cm)
- Bench knife
- Small V-tool
- Handsaw or power saw
- Woodburning tool with writing tip
- Pencil, marker, or photo-marking pencil
- Acrylic paints: black, brown, gray, green, red
- Bristle brush
- Paintbrush
- Glue
- Thumbtack or button for doorknob
- Brass tack, button, nail, or jump ring and wire for doorknob (optional)
- Toothpicks
- Clear satin spray finish
- Ruler or square
- Napkins and rags (optional)

Working with Bark

When carving fairy houses and doors, you can use a V-tool instead of a stop cut to outline components like door and window frames. This results in a softer edge that often will need to be deepened with a knife to create good shadows, but it helps to quickly lay in the forms.

Bark can sometimes chip away or break. You can fix breaks with glue, but consider allowing the natural breakage to mimic the stone face of the doorframe. A little paint works great to hide glue and breaks. If the bark face you are working on is crumbling too much, shave down a few layers to see if the bark toughens up. If not, find a different piece.

1. Draw the pattern. With a pencil, draw your whimsical doorframe onto the flat surface of the bark. Keep at least ⅛" to ¼" (3 to 6mm) or so in width for nice, chunky stones. Mark the spot for your ladybug, so you remember to leave wood for it.

2. Lower the background. Using a bench knife, lower the background around the doorframe. Cut straight down along the outside door frame edge to create a stop cut, and then remove the material around the doorframe up to the cut. Leave a nice bump of wood for the ladybug in the background.

Pattern on page 130.

3. Lower the door boards. Lower the door area inside the rock frame, so the frame stands out. Using the bench knife, cut along the inside line to create a stop cut, and then remove the material inside the doorframe. For the door handle, you can use a brass tack or carve it. If carving it, leave a bump of wood to carve later. You can also carve hinges if you are really ambitious.

4. Carve the ladybug. Cut out the ladybug and remove the wood around it down to the same level as the background. Round the bump, shaving the sharp edges to make the ladybug shape. Make a shallow cut across the top back section to separate the wings, and then poke a couple small holes for the eyes. You can use a woodburning tool to darken the head and add details, or paint them in later.

5. Carve the stone doorframe. Draw the stones. With a V-tool or knife-carved V-cuts, create the separation between the stones in the doorframe.

6. Edge the stones. Use the tip of the bench knife or a V-tool to cut the sides of the stone. This creates a more natural look. Be gentle with the background. If it gets some nicks, shave it down to clean it up.

7. Carve the door boards. Use a ruler or square to draw lines for the door boards. A square will ensure the lines are 90 degrees to the bottom edge. Mark a dot where you want the door handle. Carve the door boards using the V-tool or narrow V-cuts with the knife. Then, add further texturing with short, shallow V-cuts placed randomly along each board and along the ends. Extend the board cut with your knife under the stone doorframe to finish the line and add shadow.

8. Add depth. Bring out the texturing on the wood boards and the lines separating the boards and the stones, and then deepen the shadows around the frame itself. To get the textures and cuts to really stand out, use a woodburner or watered-down black paint.

9. Add the door handle. Use a brass tack, thumbtack, button, nail, or other ornament to create a door handle. Add a little glue before pushing it into the wood. You can also use a small jump ring on a bit of wire that's pushed into the wood to make a rustic ring handle.

10. Paint the project. Dry-brush layers of browns, from darkest to lightest, on the door boards, allowing the natural grain of the wood to show through. Dry-brush layers of gray, lightest to darkest, on the stones. Dry-brush spots of various shades of green, from darkest to lightest, on the raw outer bark on the edges and along the bottom of the stone frame. Paint the ladybug red and dot it with black. You can use a toothpick for the dots. Once the paint is dry, apply a clear topcoat as a finish.

Tip: Dry-brushing

To dry-brush, take a stiff, dry brush and dab it in paint, and then tap it on a napkin or rag until the color is almost gone. Dab lightly on your project, never brushing, only tapping. Reload the brush and tap on a rag again as needed.

Crescent Moon

BY MARY MAY

I was originally trained in classical carving, a style in which cherubs were the only frequent faces. I learned to carve faces by simply observing and studying people—and practicing a lot. Each time you carve an eye, or form a pair of lips, it brings you to the next level. How does the subtle indent around the nose blend into the cheek? How do I bring all the details in a face together to look natural? These are real challenges, and simply looking and observing people in everyday positions gives great insight. And because this smiling moon is stylized, you can relax about it not looking too "human." Just a suggestion of realism is enough to get the point across.

Tools and Materials
- Basswood, ½" to 1" (1.3cm to 2.5cm) thick: approx. 7" x 12" (17.8 x 30.5cm)
- Backer board: sized a few inches larger than pattern on all sides
- #3 gouge: 9⁄16" (14mm)
- #7 gouge: ¼" (6mm)
- V-tool: ¼" (6mm) 60-degree
- Scroll saw, band saw, or coping saw
- Pencil
- Mallet (optional)
- Clamps or bench with bench dogs
- Small rasp
- Sandpaper: 360 to 400-grit
- Carbon paper
- Colored transfer or graphite paper (optional)
- Double-sided tape
- Finish, such as boiled linseed oil or tung oil
- Hanger (optional)
- Newspaper (optional)
- Glue (optional)

Getting Started

Choose a wood variety. I carved my version in 1" (2.5cm)-thick basswood, but it can be as thin as ½" (1.3cm), as the main part of the carving is mostly on the surface. I prefer using long-handled carving gouges because these are the tools I was trained on, but you can use the tools you are comfortable with.

Prepare the blank. Transfer the design onto the wood using carbon paper. You can also use colored transfer or graphite paper. Then, cut the profile with a band saw, scroll saw, or coping saw. Clean up the saw marks with a fine rasp.

Attach the carving to a backer board with double-sided tape. Before applying the tape, I recommend testing their adhesion on scrap wood first. The backer board can be any flat board or a piece of plywood, as long as it's several inches longer than the workpiece on all sides. This allows you to work on the entire carving without having clamps in the way. Clamp the backer board down on your worktable. See the sidebar on page 19 for an alternate method for attaching the blank.

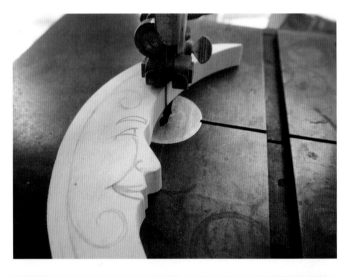

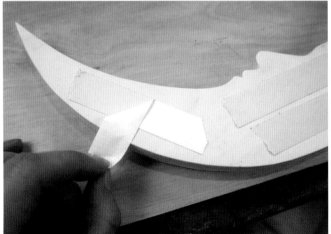

Pattern on page 132.

Alternate Backer Method

Those who prefer not to use tape can attach the blank to the backer with a layer of newspaper and glue instead. Follow these steps:

- Trace the carving blank profile onto the backer board.
- Spread a thin layer of glue on the board, within the pattern lines.
- Lay a piece of newspaper on the board.
- Spread glue on the back of the carving.
- Clamp lightly until dry.
- When you want to release the carving, simply place a flat chisel under the carving and twist gently to split the newspaper.

Instructions

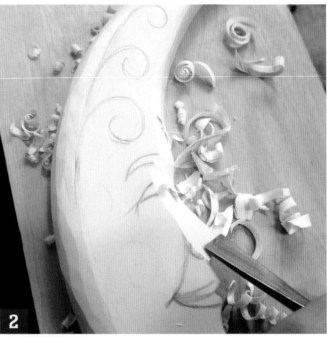

1. Soften the edges. Use a ⁹⁄₁₆" (14mm) #3 gouge to round over the back edge of the moon and the longer sections on the moon's face. The width of the rounded sections should be about ¼" (6mm). Be sure to carve correctly relative to the grain, as shown, starting in "uphill" areas, such as the center of the moon's back, and slicing "downhill" toward the pointed edges.

2. Lower the nose and lip area. Use the same tool to separate this section from the rest of the face and angle it down about ¼" (6mm). There is no need to make any defining cuts at this point, as you are just removing some of the wood to prepare for adding the details.

3. Carve the eye and cheek. Using a ¼" (6mm) 60-degree V-tool, make a sweeping curve about ³⁄₁₆" (5mm) deep to define the edge of the pudgy cheek. With the same tool, carve the upper and lower edges of the eye. To give the face a cheerful look, give the lower edge a slightly more dramatic curve. Then, switch to the ⁹⁄₁₆" (14mm) #3 gouge and lower the entire area in front of the cheek—this includes the nose and lip area—so the cheek stands out.

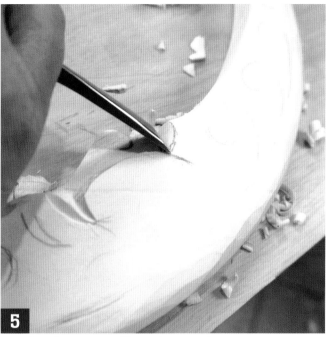

4. Draw the edge of the nostril and mouth. Then, use the ¼" (6mm) 60-degree V-tool to carve the inside of the mouth. Make this cut shallow at the outer edge of the mouth and deeper as it goes over the edge of the carving. Give it a slight upward curve to add the hint of a smile.

5. Refine the upper and lower lips. Use the ⁹⁄₁₆" (14mm) #3 gouge to clean up your cuts from Step 4.

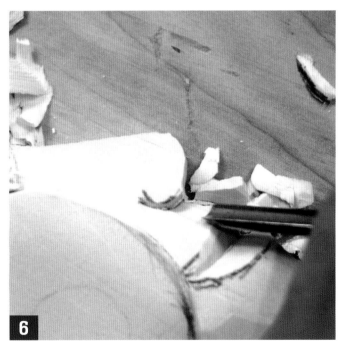

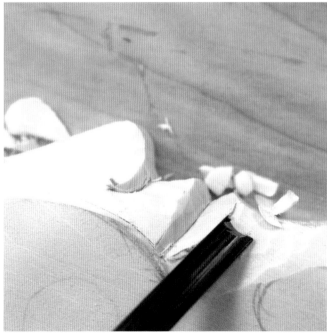

6. Carve the nose. With a ¼" (6mm) #7 gouge, define the edge of the nostril with a vertical cut. Lower and round the area between the upper lip and the nose. Then, with the same tool, hollow the section underneath the lower lip.

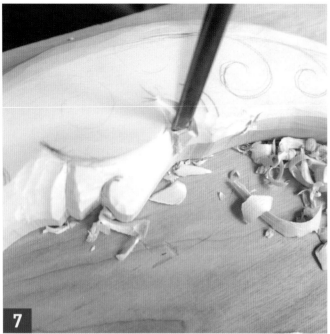

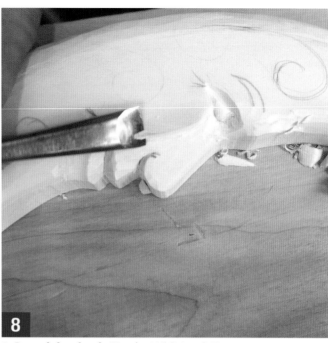

7. Refine the eye. Use the same tool to define the front edge with a vertical cut. Carve in toward that cut from the front to remove the excess, and then round over the eyeball.

8. Round the cheek. Use the ⁹⁄₁₆" (14mm) #3 gouge.

9. Carve the laugh lines. Using the ¼" (6mm) 60-degree V-tool, start at the outside corner of the eye, splaying out and fading off to three sharp points.

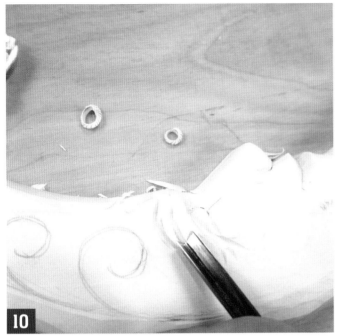

10. Carve the eyebrow. Use the same tool, keeping in mind that the curve of the eyebrow also expresses mood. Arched and round eyebrows represent a happy mood, and angled ones could show an angry mood.

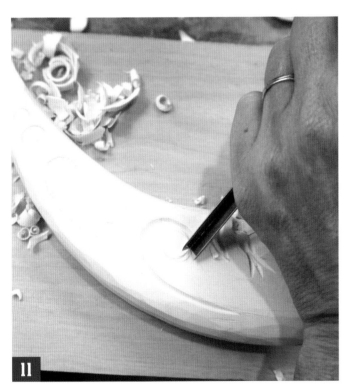

11. Add the swirls. Using the same tool, carve the curling designs on the surface of the moon. You can either push the gouge through to make these cuts, or lightly tap the top of the handle with a mallet to help get around tight curves more easily.

12. Sand and add finish to the entire piece. Using fine sandpaper (360 to 400 grit), lightly sand the carving to blend the original flat surface with the carved sections. Remove the backer board from the carving, and apply finish to front and back of the carving. I typically use a coat of boiled linseed oil or tung oil, as it gives a slight amber tint and makes the grain more visible. Display as desired; you could frame the piece or hang it directly on the wall with a sawtooth hanger.

Holiday Star

BY RICHARD EMBLING

The star is an iconic symbol of Christmastime, and is sure to put a smile on your face as it winks down from the top of the tree. I designed this charming holiday project as a twist on the classic shape. It also has a whimsical face carved in low relief, making this is an ideal project for any skill level.

Tools and Materials
- Basswood, 1" (2.5cm) thick: 5" (12.7cm) square
- Knives: rough out, detail
- #11 gouge: ⅛" (3mm)
- V-tool: ⅙" (4mm) 90-degree
- Band saw
- Pencil and pen
- Drill with bit: ⅜" (10mm)-dia.
- Acrylic paints: gold, white, yellow
- Oil paint: burnt sienna
- Paintbrushes: assorted
- Graphite paper
- Toothbrush
- Boiled linseed oil
- Toothpicks
- Wood finish
- Paper towels
- Lint-free cloth
- Mild cleaner and degreaser
- Tape: masking (optional)

Getting Started

Use graphite paper and a pencil to transfer the pattern onto the blank, making sure the design is centered on the wood. Then, use the pencil to mark the center of the bottom edge of the blank. Using a ⅜" (10mm)-dia. bit, drill down into the blank to an approximate depth of 1½" (3.8cm). Cut the star shape on a band saw. Sketch on the facial features.

Then, draw a centerline around the outer edge of the star with a pen or pencil to help you maintain symmetry as you carve.

Draw a centerline.

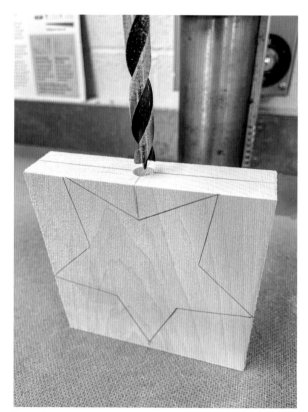

Transfer the pattern.

Pattern on
page 132.

Instructions

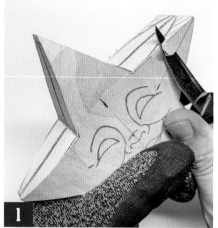

1. Rough shape the star points. Using a rough out knife, cut away from the center of the blank, and then carve toward the outer edge of each star point.

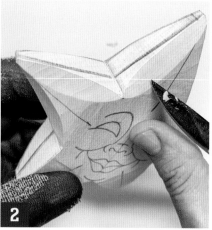

2. Taper the star points. Use the pencil or pen to draw centerlines on the front and back of each star point. Remove the corners of each point with the rough out knife to create an angled edge.

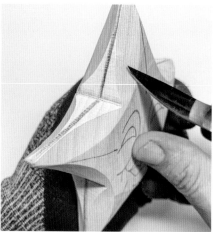

3. Redraw the facial features. Use the pencil or pen to mark in the details you may have lost during the initial stages of carving.

4. Outline the face. Use a ⅛" (4mm) 90-degree V-tool to carve all the facial features, and then deepen these cuts with a detail knife.

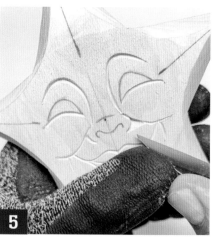

5. **Block out the nose.** Use the detail knife to make a triangular cut on either side of the nose. *Note: The nose should be the highest point on the face.*

6. Deepen the eye sockets. Use the rough out knife for this.

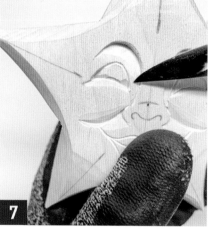

7. Round over the cheeks. Carve toward the wings of the nose using the same tool.

8. Shape the eyes. Make a triangular cut in the corners of each eye, and then round the eyes with the detail knife.

9. Refine the nose. Using a ⅛" (3mm) #11 gouge, stab cut the nose to create the nostrils. Clean up the nose and mouth area with the rough out knife.

10. Round over the lips and chin. Use the detail knife.

Tip: Additional Support

Wrap masking tape around the blunt end of a pencil to match the size of the hole underneath the star. Insert the pencil, and use it as a holding stick as you paint.

Painting and Finishing

Inspect the carving with a critical eye and remove any marks left behind from the band saw. Then, scrub the carving with a toothbrush dipped in a solution of dish soap and water to remove pen or pencil marks and dirt or oil that may have been left behind during the carving process. Allow the carving to dry fully. Then, brush on a coat of tinted boiled linseed oil. To create this, simply add a small amount of burnt sienna oil paint to a small amount boiled linseed oil and mix well. Apply this over the entire surface of the carving. After about 15 minutes, wipe away excess oil with a clean paper towel, and then allow the carving to dry overnight.

To create a slight sparkle, mix equal parts undiluted yellow and glorious gold acrylic paint. Dry-brush this color over the entire carving. When dry-brushing, keep a very small amount of paint on the brush. As you pull the brush over the carving, you want to only pick up the high points. Do this several times until you achieve the desired look. Once dry, use a toothpick to add a small star with white on each eye. Allow the paint to completely dry overnight, and then apply a coat of a wood finish of your choice. Allow it to sit for 30 minutes before buffing with a lint-free cloth.

Apply a natural finish that doesn't obscure the grain, and embellish with minimal painted details.

Twig and Leaf Drawer Handles

BY ROBERT KENNEDY

While making keepsake boxes as gifts for my family, I had the idea to spruce them up with a carved twig and leaf handle. I've since modified the design to include hardware, so the handles can be added to existing furniture, boxes, cabinets—or whatever your heart desires. After grasping the gist of the concept, make the design your own by using different woods and leaf patterns!

> ### Tools and Materials
> - Cherry, ¼" (6mm) thick: leaves, 2 each 1⅜" x 1½" (3.5 x 3.8cm)
> - Walnut, ⅝" (1.6cm) thick: twig handle, 4⅝" x 1" (11.8 x 2.5cm)
> - Carving knife
> - Skew chisel: ⅜" (10mm)
> - #1 gouges: 1⁄16" (2mm), ½" (13mm)
> - #3 gouge: ⅛" (3mm)
> - #4 gouge: 3⁄16" (5mm)
> - #9 gouge: ⅛" (3mm)
> - V-tool: 1⁄32" (1mm) 45-degree
> - Band saw
> - Drill with bits: 1⁄16" (2mm), ¾" (19mm)-dia.
> - Pencil
> - Felt-tip pen
> - Graphite paper
> - Two-part epoxy
> - Binding screws: 2 each ¾" (19mm) long
> - Finish: polyurethane
> - Grinder or belt sander (optional)

Getting Started

Cut the blanks to size, and then transfer the patterns to the blanks using graphite paper and a pencil. *Note: If you're making a handle for existing furniture, you'll have to measure the holes and shorten or lengthen the twig accordingly.* Before cutting out the twig pattern, drill the holes for the mounting hardware using a ¾" (19mm)-dia. bit. Only drill about 3⁄16" (5mm) to ¼" (6mm) deep into the bottom of the blank. Remove waste wood from all blanks using a band saw. *Note: Always wear a carving glove and thumb guard. The photos were taken without them to clearly show hand and knife positions.*

Use a drill bit to make holes for the mounting hardware.

Tip: The Skinny on Screws

Binding screws are widely available online for a reasonable price. I recommend getting a kit with different lengths, so you can suit them for the different thickness of drawers. Look for the ones with flat thin heads. If the head is thicker than 1⁄16" (2mm), you may have to sand them down a bit with a grinder or belt sander.

Pattern on page 133.

Instructions

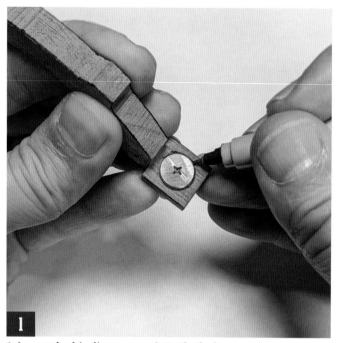

1. Insert the binding screws into the hole. Use a felt-tip pen to mark around the diameter of the head. Then, remove the screw and use a ⅛" (3mm) #3 gouge to make a downward stop cut along the circumference of the mark. Go only as far as the thickness of the screw head, in this case about ¹⁄₁₆" (2mm).

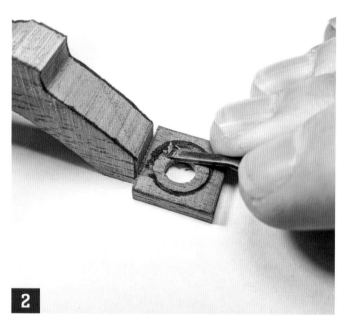

2. Level the edge. Using a ¹⁄₁₆" (2mm) #1 gouge, cut from the edge of the hole to the stop cut along the circumference. Then, reinsert the binding screw. The head of the screw should sit flush or just below the surface.

3. Place the bottom of the leaf onto the twig blank. Making sure it's centered, use a pencil to outline the edge of the twig blank onto the leaf.

4. Create a shelf for the twig blank. Using a ½" (13mm) #1 gouge, make a downward stop cut along the marks you drew in Step 3. Carve into it to a depth of about ⅛" (3mm). *Note: Do not try to achieve the ⅛" (3mm) depth all at once—you will likely split the leaf.* Lower the depth a little at a time. Once finished, the leaf should socket flush into the twig. Repeat Steps 1–4 for the other side.

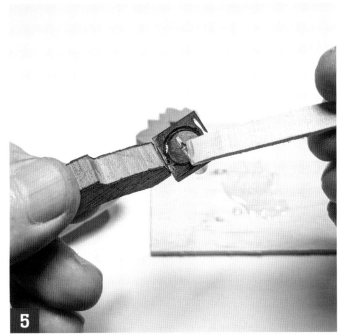

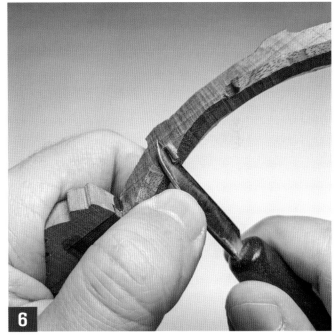

5. Insert the binding screws back into the twig. Apply two-part epoxy to the twig and leaf socket, press them together, and wipe away any squeeze-out. Repeat on the other side. Make sure the binding screws are straight. Once the epoxy sets, these will not move. Let sit overnight.

6. Shape the twig. Using a carving knife, begin rounding the underside of the twig, working with the grain toward the center. It's best to take a little off at a time to avoid tear-out. Near the center, you'll have to do a bit of back and forth, cutting in both directions to achieve a clean cut where the grain meets.

7. Mark the stumps on the top side of the twig. Then, using a ⅛" (3mm) #9 gouge, cut toward the center of the circumference. Work with the grain along the sides. Repeat for the other stump. Use the carving knife to taper the end of the twig into the leaf, working with the grain. You may have to switch back to the ⅛" (3mm) #9 gouge to clean up the cuts around the stumps.

 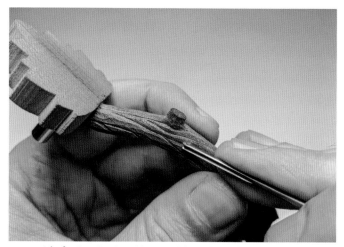

8. Draw bark lines on the twig. Reference photos of real-life twigs or step outside for inspiration. Use a ¹⁄₃₂" (1mm) 45-degree V-tool to cut in the lines. Then, go back over the lines with the same tool, angling it slightly to the left and right, to round the lines.

9. Add the leaf details. Drill four holes on each leaf using a ¹⁄₁₆" (2mm)-dia. bit. You don't need to go all the way through—just about ³⁄₁₆" (5mm). Mark around the edge of the leaf about ⅛" (3mm) from the bottom. Draw a centerline from the tip of the leaf to the twig.

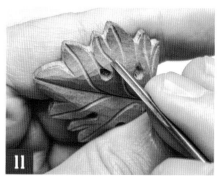

11. Add the leaf veins. Mark them with the pen or pencil, and then use the ⅟₃₂" (1mm) 45-degree V-tool to cut them in, working outward from the center. Then, using the ⅛" (3mm) #9 gouge, make small, concave cuts between the leaf veins and the edge of the leaf. This adds some shadow and visual interest.

10. Shape the outer edge of the leaf. Use a ³⁄₁₆" (5mm) #4 gouge, working from the back to the tip, bringing the edge down to the line. Then, use the ⅟₃₂" (1mm) 45-degree V-tool to cut the centerline. Use a ⅜" (10mm) skew chisel to round any hard edges. The shape of the leaf should look like an open book when viewed from the front. Repeat on the other side.

12. Bevel the outside edge of the leaf. Use the ⅜" (10mm) skew chisel to round the outside edge in toward the eyelets. The bevel should be about ⅟₁₆" (2mm) or less. Then, bevel the eyelets with the ⅛" (3mm) #9 gouge, angled downward toward the center. Flip the leaf over and use the ⅜" (10mm) skew chisel to bevel the underside of the leaf up until it nearly meets the bevel on top.

13. Add embellishment. Use the ⅟₃₂" (1mm) 45-degree V-tool to cut in a couple of concentric circles in the top of each stump. Work slowly, being careful not to remove too much wood at once. I keep my thumb pressed against the edge of the stump and the side of the V-tool, and I spin the twig rather than the tool. Repeat for the other stump. Add a finish; I applied four even coats of clear semigloss spray lacquer, letting the finish dry between coats. Attach to a drawer or cabinet after the finish dries and use!

Sailboat

BY DUSTIN STRENKE

One thing I greatly respect about shallow relief is that one miscut or lapse in focus can ruin the carving, and correcting mistakes is much more difficult due to the lack of depth available. For me, it's satisfying to create dynamic depth knowing that the deepest part of the carving is only a fraction of an inch below the surface. Deceiving the eye is the challenge. This design was inspired by a stained-glass decoration that was once displayed on my grandparents' porch. I remember seeing it as a child during visits and being struck by its uniqueness.

Getting Started

Choose your material; I used a 2" (5.1cm)-thick block of pine, but you could use a thinner piece, if desired. Transfer the design onto the wood with graphite or carbon transfer paper and a pencil or pen. Make sure all your tools are sharpened before you begin and secure the wood block with clamps or a vise.

Tools and Materials
- Basswood or pine, ½" to 2" (1.3 to 5.1cm) thick: 8" (20.3cm) square
- Skew chisel: ½" (13mm)
- #2 gouge: ½" (13mm)
- #3 gouge: ³⁄₁₆" (5mm)
- #5 gouge: ½" (13mm)
- #7 gouges: ⁵⁄₃₂" (4mm), ⁹⁄₁₆" (14mm)
- #8 gouge: ³⁄₈" (10mm)
- V-tool: ¼" (6mm) 60-degree
- Pen or pencil
- Mallet
- Clamps or vise
- File: mini angled
- Foam brush
- Graphite or carbon transfer paper
- Sandpaper: assorted grits to 320
- Paper towels
- Oil-based stain: natural
- Polyurethane: warm satin

Instructions

1. Carve the rough outline. Using a ¼" (6mm) 60-degree V-tool and, if desired, a mallet, outline the outside edges of the sailboat and birds that touch the sky and water. Go slowly and make sure you're carving on the correct side of the line. Make multiple passes until you've reached your desired depth. Remember, the more depth created, the more material you'll have to shape later. This also makes it easier to correct mistakes if necessary. For now, hold off on outlining the bottom section of the boat where it touches the water.

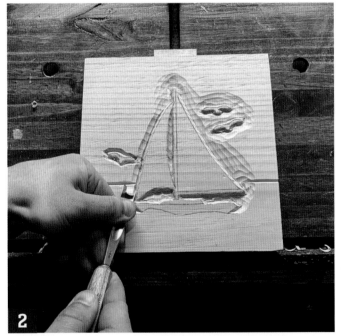

2. Taper the background. Using a ⁹⁄₁₆" (14mm) #7 gouge, carve along the outside edge of the sailboat and birds, creating a gradual taper toward the design that descends by 1" to 2" (2.5cm to 5.1cm). This gives the carving depth without having to lower the entire background.

Pattern on page 134.

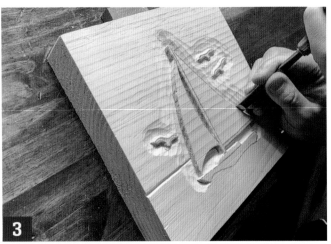

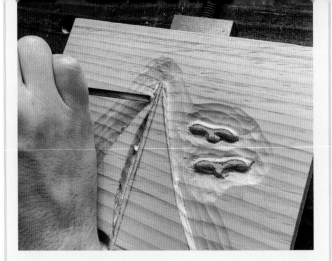

3. Refine the boat outline. Carve vertical stop cuts along the areas you outlined in Step 1, using a gouge that best matches the curvature of the design. It's good to have a variety of sweeps, so you can best match different areas of the design. I primarily used a ½" (13mm) #2 gouge and a ³⁄₁₆" (5mm) #3 gouge, as well as a ½" (13mm) #5 gouge and a ½" (13mm) skew chisel.

Tip: Take Care

Carve very carefully around the vertical post and the three corners of the left sail. These areas are prone to breakage if too much pressure is applied. Use small gouges and go slowly.

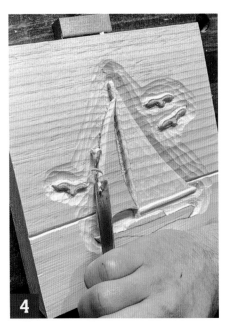

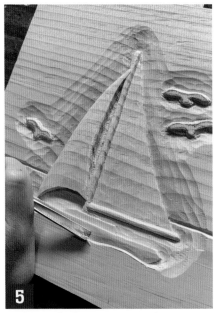

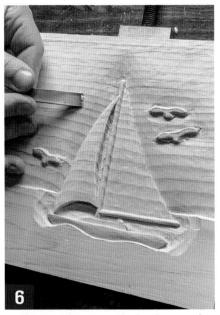

4. Shape the sails and posts. Using the ⁹⁄₁₆" (14mm) #7 gouge, carve the right sail almost to the depth of the background taper. This gives you the most wood possible to shape the posts and left sail. Make sure your strokes are consistent and the depths are even throughout the sail. Then, using the ³⁄₁₆" (5mm) #3 gouge, round the vertical and horizontal posts. Using the ½" (13mm) #2 gouge, shape the left sail by carving a slight taper, getting deeper as you move left. This gives the sail a curved appearance. If desired, use the same tool to soften the gouge strokes made when carving the sails. The sails need to have a smooth look, so softening them up now makes the sanding step easier at the end.

5. Shape the boat. Separate the upper and lower sections of the boat with stop cuts, using the same tool as in Step 4. Carve the upper section almost to the depth of the vertical post. Then, using the ¼" (6mm) 60-degree V-tool, outline where the bottom of the boat encounters the water. Carve above the line this time, so the boat appears to be floating. Carve away that hard line created by the V-tool by carving a slight taper toward the water with the ½" (13mm) #2 gouge.

6. Clean and texture the background. Add a subtle texture to the sky to better blend the uncarved and carved areas using the ½" (13mm) #5 gouge. Go over it again with the ½" (13mm) #2 gouge to soften the carving strokes. This is also the time to clean up any nicks or gouge marks made near the sailboat during shaping. Stain will highlight any imperfections, so it's important to identify and fix problem areas now.

7. Clean and texture the water. Using the ⁹⁄₁₆" (14mm) #7 gouge, carve horizontal and gradual S-shaped strokes to create waves. Use larger gouges for the waves up close, and then change to smaller gouges as you carve the distant waves to establish proper dimension and depth. Make sure your strokes are clean because you won't be sanding this part later.

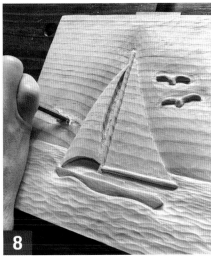

8. Carve the birds. Using the ³⁄₁₆" (5mm) #3 gouge and a ⁵⁄₃₂" (4mm) #7 gouge, carve vertical stop cuts around the birds. The birds are small and delicate, so it's important to carve slowly and take care so the wings don't break. Again, using the same gouges, shape the birds by tapering the bodies. It's not critical to get the birds identical or add too much detail here; simply the suggestion of birds will do.

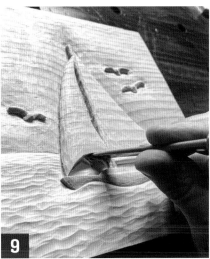

9. Undercut in strategic areas. Using a gouge that best matches the curve of the design, carve a nearly vertical stop cut, but instead hold the gouge at a more aggressive angle, allowing you to carve underneath the design. This does not have to be applied to the entire carving, only in strategic spots to emphasize those areas and separate them from the layer behind them. Undercut the areas where the sails touch the water and sky and where the top sections of the boat touch the water. Do not undercut the bottom of the boat, as that would detract from this area's realism.

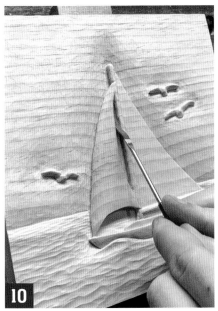

10. Refine and sand. Smooth the sails to get rid of the gouge strokes, using 220- and 320-grit sandpaper. If desired, soften the sky texture, as well. A mini file works well to clean up the tight area between the sail and vertical post. At this stage, look for and fix accidental plunge marks or imperfections. Sometimes sanding is all that is needed, but if the plunge is deep, you may need to fix it with a gouge.

11. Add finish. I used a foam brush and a natural-color, oil-based stain, but there are several stain options and application methods available. Apply stain to the entire project, including the sides and back, and wipe off any extra with a paper towel. Let it dry, and then apply a protective finish such as polyurethane.

Floating Leaf

BY D.L. MILLER

A freshly fallen leaf floating down a stream is a true sign that seasonal changes are upon us. At first look, our focus is on the brilliance of the leaf's surface, but at second glance, we might start to pick up on the details of the stream bed under it, blanketed with smooth pebbles. I set out to replicate this iconic symbol of fall by combining clear resin with a simple low-relief image.

Giving an illusion of depth is both the challenge and reward of low-relief carving. The introduction of resin can greatly enhance the illusion. This project will teach you basic techniques that can later be applied to larger, more advanced designs.

Tools and Materials
- Basswood panel, 1" (2.5cm) thick: 12" (30.5cm) square
- Hobby knife or thin, straight-bladed knife
- #3 gouge: ⅜" (10mm)
- V-tool: ¼" (6mm) 70-degree
- Chisel of choice
- Small level
- Ruler
- Pencil
- Graphite paper
- Acrylic paints, such as cadmium yellow, crimson red, Mars black, ultramarine blue, and white
- #12 round paintbrush
- Two-part clear epoxy kit (16 fl. oz.)
- Clear plastic cup
- Disposable craft stick
- Small spray bottle of isopropyl alcohol
- Waxed paper
- Disposable gloves
- Disposable plastic sheet

Getting Started

Choose a variety of wood. For this project, I used a 4" (10.2cm) square space centered on a 12" (30.5cm) square basswood panel. Using a panel larger than your carving surface will allow for safe handling during the carving process as well as provide a ready-made gallery-style frame when finished. Transfer the pattern onto the center of the panel using graphite transfer paper and a pencil (or another method of your choice).

Instructions

1. Create the outlines. Using a hobby knife or a straight-bladed carving knife of your choice, create stop cuts along the lines for the square frame and leaf outline, ⅜" (1cm) deep. It's helpful to use a ruler as a guide along the straight stop cuts.

Pattern on page 135.

Carve your leaf into a larger square of wood to create a ready-made frame.

2. Lower the background. Using a chisel or a ⅜" (10mm) #3 gouge, begin removing the background material between leaf and frame, carving with the grain. Bring down the background by roughly ⅜" (1cm).

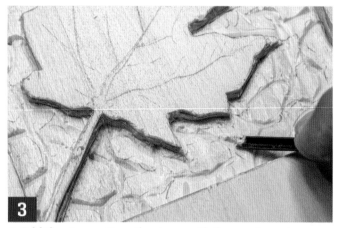

3. Add the stones. Draw the stones with the pencil, varying their size and shape for an organic look. Then, use a ¼" (6mm) 70-degree V-tool to create definition between the stones.

5. Shape the stem. With the same gouge, gently slope the stem downward toward the frame. This will help to give the floating leaf a more realistic appearance, as some parts will naturally sink lower in the "water." Then, with the ¼" (6mm) 70-degree V-tool, add the leaf vein details.

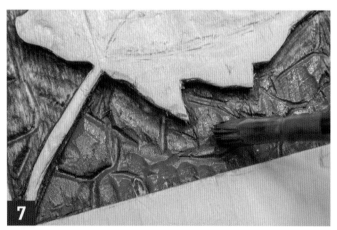

7. Mix Mars black with white to create a dark gray. Dilute the mixture until it is around 70 percent paint and 30 percent water, and then paint on the pebble background, the interior of the frame edge, and the edges of the leaf and stem. Do not try to cover every element thickly; it is better to show random thick and thin areas, as this will give the pebbles a more mottled appearance.

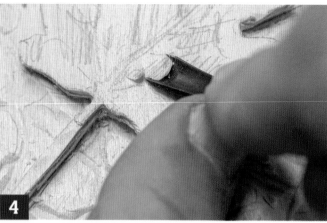

4. Carve the surface of the leaf. Using a shallow gouge, such as the ⅜" (10mm) #3, create the leaf's surface by starting from the outside of the leaf's edge and moving toward the center leaf veins. Remove just a small amount of material. *Note: Make sure not to remove any material from the leaf's edge. The high points along the leaf's perimeter will keep it from being flooded by resin as you pour later.*

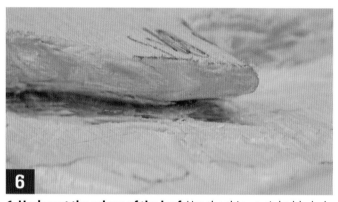

6. Undercut the edges of the leaf. Use the thin, straight-bladed knife. Do not undercut the stem. Inspect your carving and add any final details.

8. Paint the leaf base coat. Mix crimson red with cadmium yellow to create a vibrant orange, and then brush the surface of the leaf and stem with this color. Vary the tone by blending in more crimson red and cadmium yellow in places. Let dry.

9. Add the leaf vein details. Mix cadmium yellow with a small amount of ultramarine blue to create a pale green, and then use this to carefully paint on the leaf vein details.

10. Prepare the surface for resin. Before adding resin, place the finished piece on a flat surface. Do not pour any resin until your panel is level from all directions; I used a bubble level to check all directions—diagonally as well as along the top and sides. Then, cover your working surface with waxed paper or a disposable plastic sheet, and put on gloves before mixing.

11. Add the resin. Using a two-part epoxy, mix a total of 5 oz., following the manufacturer's instructions. The instructions will provide details on exact mixing rations, which vary per brand but are often 1:1; they will also include details on working and curing times. Be sure to follow all safety instructions when mixing and pouring resin. Slowly pour your mixed resin into one corner of the frame, allowing the resin to slowly travel around and fill the background. Pour a small amount to start, and then slowly pour a little more, carefully watching the resin level rise at all four corners. Pour a little at a time until the resin has reached the edges of the leaf.

12. Add the water droplets. Take a sharpened craft stick and dip it into the remaining resin in your mixing cup. You can create the appearance of water droplets on the surface of the leaf by letting a small drop of resin drip off the tip of the sharpened craft stick. For this piece, I added about eight drops of various sizes.

13. Remove air bubbles. Even with careful pouring, small air bubbles will appear on the surface of the resin, giving it a cloudy appearance. To eliminate them, spray a mist of isopropyl alcohol on the surface. Let the resin set for at least 24 hours (or the time listed in the manufacturer's instructions) before moving the carving. Display as desired.

Tip: Take Your Time

Slow pouring will prevent additional air bubbles in the resin, as well as lessen the likelihood of overflow.

Frank the Sweet Greeter

BY JANET BOLYARD

Frank the Sweet Greeter is the first decoration to come out of the closet every Halloween at our house. Our family enjoys filling him up with sweets, and we enjoy his winning smile. Not only does he help us decorate our house, but he also becomes a great greeter and candy holder for trick-or-treaters on the big night. He helps start conversations and generates many smiles each year.

With the pattern for Frank, I've included extra patterns so you can embellish your box and make it your own. You can even modify the pattern for Frank. Place a sheet of tracing paper over the original pattern and change the nose, add different clothes, or even have a little critter peeking out of his bag. Just use your imagination and have fun with it.

Transfer the pattern to your blank.

Tools and Materials

- Basswood or poplar, ¾" (1.9cm) thick: Frank, 7½" x 26" (19.1 x 66cm)
- Plywood, ⅜" (1cm) thick: sides, 2 each 5⅞" x 7½" (14.9 x 19.1cm); bottom, 7⅛" x 7⅝" (18.1 x 19.4cm); front, 5⅞" x 8⅛" (14.9 x 20.6cm)
- Detail knife
- #3 gouge: ⅜" (10mm)
- #6 gouge: 5⁄16" (8mm)
- V-tool: ¼" (6mm) 70-degree
- Scroll or jig saw
- Circular or table saw
- Pencil
- Blue ink pen
- Pin nailer (optional)
- Clamps
- Sandpaper: 220-grit
- Graphite paper
- Wood glue
- Brown paper bag
- Pre-stain coordinator
- Spray satin lacquer
- Masking tape
- Acrylic paints: black (box, hair, pupil, lettering, sock stripes), black plum (coat, candy), cherry red (shoes, patches, lollipop), gray (metal studs, metal straps), orange (shirt, treat bag, box details, candy corn), tomato red (pink cheeks), white (eyes, metal details, shoes, shoelaces, candy corn, lollipop stripe, lollipop stick, candy details), yellow (fingernails, patch dots, candy corn, strap), yellow green (skin)
- Paintbrushes: ¼" (6mm), ½" (1.3cm) sword-shaped; ¼" (6mm) angled shader; #3 liner; #4 round
- Metal ruler

Getting Started

Cut the pieces to size. Then, sand everything with 220-grit sandpaper. Center the pattern on the blanks, and secure it to the wood with a piece of tape on the top. Slide a piece of graphite paper (which is easier to remove than carbon paper) under the pattern, with the shiny side facing the wood. Trace the pattern onto the blank with a colored pen (so you can see where you've already traced). Lift the pattern periodically to make sure you're transferring the entire pattern to the blank.

Patterns on
pages 45 and 134.

Carving and Assembling

Cut Frank's outline with a scroll saw or jig saw. Cut the other components with a table saw or circular saw. Carve Frank before assembling the box. Treat Frank as a relief carving. I carve him using just four tools. After you finish carving, glue and clamp the candy box together. Use a pin nailer to secure the joints, if desired. Sand the edges with 220-grit sandpaper.

Finishing

Before painting, seal the wood, so the paint and brush flow across the wood smoothly, especially for wood as porous as basswood. I use a pre-stain conditioner. This water-based product is easy to use, dries clear (without yellowing), and is easy to clean up.

Now, paint the project. I dilute 1 drop of paint with five drops of water. If you need the paint to be darker, apply more coats. If the paint is too thick, it will cover the wood and make it look like plastic. To soften the face, I add a small amount of diluted tomato red to the cheeks and lips. To break up the all-black look, I use black plum for the jacket.

After the paint dries, apply three coats of spray satin lacquer. Buff between coats with a crumpled-up brown paper bag.

Paint and seal the finished piece.

TIPS

Prevent Warping

To keep a board from warping or cupping, especially when you plan to apply a water-based paint or sealer, score the back of the carving with a series of diagonal V-tool cuts. I use a metal ruler to make neat and orderly lines. Take a light pass to reduce tear out, and then make a second, deeper cut. Depending on the thickness of the blank, these cuts should be ⅛" (3mm) to ¼" (6mm) deep.

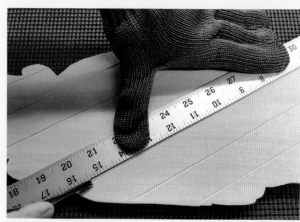

Score the back of the wood to prevent warping.

Carving High Relief

To create a 3D look for this relief carving, I make deep cuts. The deep cuts under and around Frank's nose make it stand out and give him more character.

Deep cuts help lend a 3D effect.

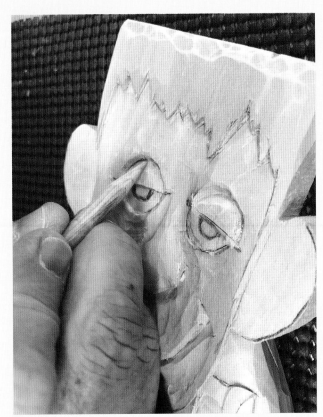
Burnish the eyes and ears for a more refined look.

Smoothing the Eyes and Ears

After carving the eyes and ears, I burnish these areas with a sharpened birch dowel. This helps clean up the carving and refines the carved angles. To make a burnisher, cut a ¼" (6mm)-diameter birch dowel down to about the length of a pencil, and sharpen the end in a pencil sharpener.

A Useful Tool

After a detail knife, I use a ⅜" (10mm) #3 gouge more than any other tool for this project. This tool has just enough of a sweep that I can maneuver it through the wood easily. I use it upside down to round sharp edges.

A #3 gouge is invaluable for this project.

Frank the Sweet Greeter Pattern

Photocopy at 200%

Flower Barrette

BY IVAN GOVAERTS

I always used to make my wooden barrettes the classic way, with a metal clip in back. Then, at an art fair, I met a woman with very thick hair—hair so thick that the barrette wouldn't hold it all! Soon, this curved clip was born.

The lotus flower is regarded in many cultures, especially in Eastern religions, as symbolic of enlightenment and rebirth. Its characteristics are a perfect analogy for the human condition: even with roots in the dirtiest waters, this plant can produce a beautiful flower. I used the lathe to turn the pin on my lotus barrette, but you could carve it instead, if desired. The finish is an eco-friendly water-based varnish, which holds up to hair grease and common styling products. Enjoy!

Tools and Materials
- Maple, 1⅝" (4.1cm) thick: curve, 2⅜" x 4 ¹¹⁄₁₆" (6 x 11.9cm)
- Maple, ¾" (1.9cm) square: pin, approx. 8" (20.3cm) long
- Detail knife
- Straight gouge
- Small gouges (optional)
- V-scorp
- Gouge scorp
- V-tool of your choice
- Band saw
- Scroll saw
- Lathe (optional)
- Drill press with bit: ⁹⁄₃₂" (7mm)-dia.
- Pencil
- Sandpaper: 80, 120, 400, 600-grit
- Carbon or graphite transfer paper
- Tack cloth
- Spray adhesive or repositionable glue stick
- Finish, such as water-based varnish: satin

Getting Started

Choose a variety of wood; I used maple, but you can use whatever wood you like. I recommend hardwoods for increased durability, however. *Note: For carving, I use a detail knife, straight gouge, V-scorp, and gouge scorp, but you can use some small gouges and a V-tool of your choice as an alternative option.*

Instructions

1. Cut the basic shape. Use the template to draw a curved line along the side of the wood and cut the side view with a band saw. Apply the pattern on the concave side along the length of the grain using repositionable spray adhesive or a glue stick. Then, using pieces of scrap wood to keep the blank level, cut the shape of the lotus (the top view) on a scroll saw. Then, using graphite transfer paper and a pencil, draw the lotus design on the convex side of the blank. Remove pattern from the concave side.

2. Drill the holes for the pin. Start by bracing the blank, convex-side-down, against the work surface, and begin to drill a ⁹⁄₃₂" (7mm) hole straight down into the wood. Once the drill grabs into the wood, tilt the workpiece in the direction you want the pin to go, and then drill the rest of the hole at that angle. When you drill a hole on the other side, make sure it matches the first in angle. Do not drill too close to the edge of the wood; otherwise, the piece may split. Once both holes are drilled, carefully take the blank in your hand and clean them up with the same bit.

Pattern on page 135.

3. Round the inside. To give the piece a sense of lightness, thin down the inside (or back) of the piece with a detail knife, tapering the edges of the leaves toward each point and carving off saw marks over the entire surface. Do not overcut the petals here, as they can become fragile.

4. Begin to separate the top details. With a V-tool of your choice, carve along the central V and any details within it. Clean up your cuts with the detail knife.

5. Refine Section A. Bring down the level of the wood within the central V using a gouge of your choice, and then round this area over with the detail knife. Using the same tool, deepen the cut between the two outer petals and the bottom of the V. Bring down the petals even lower by scooping out the centers with a scorp or a gouge of your choice. Keep the upper edges of the petals mostly untouched for now.

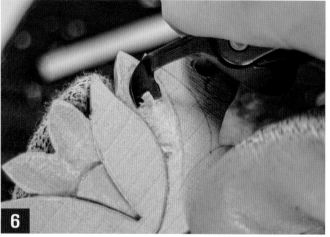

6. Shape Section C. Wait to carve Section B next to the middle section until later. For this next group of petals, follow the same method and tools as for Section A. Switch to a smaller gouge at the base.

7. Add more details. With the detail knife, distinguish the ball at the very base of the carving (Section F), and then round it over with a series of small slices. Only the front has to be completely round. Then, shape Section D, hollowing the petals as in Steps 5 and 6. Deepen the bases of these petals, so they sit below Section C.

8. Define Section E. Make cuts with the V-tool and detail knife around the volute, and then deepen the part between the volute and petals with the detail knife.

9. Shape the bottom leaves in Section C. Hollow their centers with the scorp or a small gouge of your choice.

10. Round the large petals. With the detail knife, carve the outside edges of Section B. Leave the tops fairly flat. Then, round over the volutes in Section E completely with the same tool.

11. Sand the carving. I usually sand most of my carvings, but you could leave the carved facets prominent, if desired. Start with 80-grit and then move progressively up through the grits, from 120 to 320 to 400 (and even 600, if desired). Wipe off the dust with a tack cloth.

Making the Pin

Cut the blank to size and round it using the knife or a lathe. The pin should be long enough to go through the two holes of the barrette and protrude around 1" (2.5cm) on either side. Make sure the pin does not fit too tightly in the holes. Carve the round finial on one end, taper the other to a blunted point, and then sand through the grits, removing excess dust.

Finishing

I finished this project with three coats of a satin, eco-friendly, water-based varnish—the same you might use on wooden floors. I use this because it protects against the grease of the hair and head, as well as light rain. However, you could use a different finish, if desired.

Miniature Acanthus

BY MARY MAY

When I travelled to Europe as a teenager, I was swept away by the carved, scrolling leaves that adorned the furniture and architecture of churches and cathedrals. As a new student of historic design, I did not know what to call this decorative motif. But I soon discovered its name—the acanthus (pronounced uh-kan-thuhs).

Many carvings I make are on a larger architectural scale, so it was fun to carve a tiny version of that beautiful leaf for this project. You can use the finished product in earrings, pendants, brooches, and more.

Tools and Materials
- Mahogany, ¼" (6mm) thick: small earring, 2 each 1⅛" x 1⅞" (2.9 x 4.8cm)
- Backer board, ¼" (6mm) thick: 6" (15.2cm) square
- Rough out knife
- Detail knife
- #3 gouges: ⅛" (3mm), ¼" (6mm)
- #5 gouge: ¼" (6mm)
- #9 gouge: ³⁄₁₆" (5mm)
- V-tool, ⅛" (3mm): 60-degree
- Flat chisel of choice
- Coping saw or scroll saw with blades: #1 reverse-tooth
- Pencil
- Riffler or needle files
- Drill with bit: ¹⁄₃₂" (1mm)-dia.
- Needle-nose pliers (optional)
- Vise (optional)
- Graphite transfer paper or carbon paper
- Double-sided tape
- Jewelry glue or two-part epoxy (optional)
- Finish, such as boiled linseed oil or clear shellac
- Eye pins (optional)
- Wire, thin (optional)
- String, cord, or chain (optional)
- Pin or barrette (optional)
- Solvent

Getting Started

Transfer the outline of the design, including the scroll, onto the wood using graphite transfer paper or carbon paper. I do not transfer all lines at this stage because many will be carved away during shaping. Make sure the grain runs vertically, as this will provide necessary strength to the leaf. *Note: If you choose to carve a pair of earrings, the second leaf will need to be reversed. Use the mirror-image version of the pattern for this purpose.*

Make the blank. Cut the design with a coping saw or scroll saw with a small blade, such as a #1 reverse-tooth. Make sure to cut directly on the line, making your cuts as clean and accurate as possible. Clean up any edges to remove saw cut marks; I used small riffler or needle files.

Transfer the design to the blank and cut it out.

Pattern on
page 135.

Instructions

1. Attach the blank to a smooth backer board with double-sided tape. I used plywood, but you can use any scrap wood you have lying around. Because this piece is small, I chose to use a backer rather than holding it in my hand; this ensures greater safety and control. With a rough out knife, cut away any excess tape so that woodchips won't stick to it.

2. Cut the scroll. Follow the line you drew in on page 50, making a vertical stop cut with a ³⁄₁₆" (5mm) #9 gouge. Gently rock the tool rather than driving it forcefully into the wood. Switch to a ¼" (6mm) #5 gouge as the scroll opens up. The cut should be around ¹⁄₃₂" (1mm) deep at the inside of the scroll and around ¹⁄₁₆" (2mm) deep as it unfurls. **(CAUTION! The wood could easily split if you press too hard—especially when making cuts along the grain.)**

3. Begin to shape the leaf. With a ¼" (6mm) #3 gouge, make an angled cut that starts at the edge of the scroll and ends on the side of the leaf. This cut should be ⅛" (3mm) deep where it meets the scroll. Essentially, you'll be creating a ramp or "slide" down from the center of the scroll to its natural end, on one edge of the leaf.

4. Shape the scroll. With the ¼" (6mm) #5 gouge, make a continuous cut starting from the outer edge of the scroll, angling down to meet the vertical cuts you made in Step 2. The depth of these cuts gradually gets shallower as you reach the inside curve.

5. Round the outer edges of the leaf. Using the ¼" (6mm) #3 gouge—bevel-side-down so the edges don't catch the wood—gently round over all the outer edges of the leaf, bringing them down around ⅛" (3mm). Round the entire surface of the leaf into the edges, so none of the original flat surfaces remain.

6. Draw the lobes. Referring to the pattern, draw the upper edges of each lobe. Because of the curved surface of the leaf, it is difficult to transfer these using carbon or graphite paper, so I drew the lines by hand.

7. Carve the central vein. Using a ⅛" (3mm) 60-degree V-tool, carve the center vein. Start this cut from the highest point in the center of the leaf, and then carve downhill in both directions. Do not slice all the way to the tip of the leaf or it will give the appearance that the leaf splits. Instead, stop ⅛" (3mm) from the tip of the leaf, letting the tool gradually come out of the wood to leave a nice, sharp point where this vein line ends.

9. Round the lobes. Using the ¼" (6mm) #3 gouge, carve down the sections of the lobes at a slight angle so each appears to be going underneath the lobe above it. *Note: The lobes closer to the scroll will overlap those farther from it.* Carve down about ¹⁄₁₆" (2mm) along the outer edge, going shallower as you approach the center of the leaf.

11. Add serration to the lobes. Using the ¼" (6mm) #5 gouge, make small notch cuts on each tiny serration of the leaf. To do this, first make a vertical cut along the notch in the leaf, and then make a second one further toward the tip of the leaf at a slight angle to cut out a tiny, triangular chip. This is a very small cut, but it will go far in creating a more 3D look. Draw all remaining vein lines in each lobe.

8. Define the lobes. Using a ⅛" (3mm) #3 gouge and the ¼" (6mm) #3 gouge, make vertical cuts directly into the lines you drew in Step 6 to define the upper (overlapping) edges of each lobe. Make these cuts ¹⁄₁₆" (2mm) deep at the outer edges of the leaf, and gradually shallower as they reach the center. Again, make these cuts by gently rocking the tool, as any harsh, vertical cuts can easily split the wood.

10. Round the leaf into the vein. Using the same tool, slightly round the leaf down to the central vein that you cut in Step 7. Do this on both sides of the V-cut. By removing the sharp edges of the vein line, you'll give the leaf a softer appearance.

12. Carve the remaining vein lines. Use the ⅛" (3mm) 60-degree V-tool, making the center veins slightly deeper than the secondary ones. When making these cuts, start near the center vein of the leaf and move downhill toward the outer edges to avoid ugly chip-out. Start shallow and end shallow, resulting in nice, sharp cuts that don't reach the end of the lobe at any point.

13. Refine the scroll. Using the ¼" (6mm) #3 gouge, soften the outer edge of the scroll. Start at the top of the curve, as shown in the photo, and then turn and carve from that point in the other direction to complete that edge, always making sure you are carving downhill.

14. Undercut the leaf. Using a combination of the gouges you used previously, make angled undercuts along the edge of the carving so that the original vertical edges are not as visible. I made angle cuts at roughly a 30-degree angle, as more aggressive angles are difficult to make without flipping the piece over.

15. Add the finishing touches. Using a flat chisel, place the blade between the carving and the backer board, and gently lift and twist until the double-sided tape releases. If it is difficult to release, brush solvent along the edge of the carving and the tape will release more easily. Then, add finish; I prefer boiled linseed oil or shellac because it brings out a nice sheen in the wood.

Finishing the Design

Now that your leaf is finished, you can transform it into a number of jewelry pieces. *Note: Jewelry-making materials can be purchased from any craft store or jewelry-making supply store.*

Adding the Eye Pin

Brace the carving in a vise and drill a tiny hole in the top. Make sure the hole is slightly larger than the eye pin to be inserted. Secure the eye pin in place using epoxy or jeweler's glue. You could also cut a small length of thin wire with needle-nose pliers and twist the end to form a loop.

Earrings: Using needle-nose pliers, gently open the wire loop in the earring hook, connect the two loops, and gently close the wire loop with the pliers.

Necklace: Insert a chain, string of leather, or length of ribbon or cloth through the loop.

Brooch or Barrette: Glue a pin or barrette onto the back of the carving. Make sure the finish that you chose does not prevent the glue from sticking (or apply a finish after you glue this on).

Drill a hole for the eye pin.

Intermediate Projects

Honeybee

BY LUCY FOX

Did you know that honeybees and other pollinators are the reason roughly a third of our food exists? These amazing creatures are the tiny "farmers" of the natural world. This particular bee is carved in basswood (called limewood in the United Kingdom), and I've centered the design in a bowl of scooped-out wood. With some careful undercutting, it is possible to give the bee and flowers a lovely, realistic lift, which really brings it to life—a great way to hone your relief carving skills.

Tools and Materials

- Basswood, ½" (1.3cm) thick: 7⅞" (20cm) square
- Chisel: 5⁄16" (8mm)
- #2 gouge: 9⁄16" (14mm)
- #3 gouges: ⅛" (3mm), ¼" (6mm), 9⁄16" (14mm), ¾" (19mm)
- #5 gouge: 3⁄16" (5mm)
- #6 gouge: 3⁄16" (5mm)
- #7 gouges: ¼" (6mm), 5⁄16" (8mm)
- Micro gouge: 1⁄32" (1mm)
- V-tool: 3⁄16" (5mm) 60-degree
- Pencil
- Ruler
- Mallet
- Compass
- Vise
- Carbon or graphite transfer paper
- Sandpaper: 180 to 320-grit
- Beeswax
- Buffing cloth
- Background punch
- Brush
- Old toothbrush
- Hair dryer

1. Position the pattern stock with the grain running vertically. With a ruler, draw a cross from corner to corner to determine the center point. Using a compass, draw a circle with a radius of 3⅛" (7.9cm) centered on that point. Position the image on the wood, and transfer it with carbon or graphite paper and a pencil. Secure the wood to your carving surface in a vise.

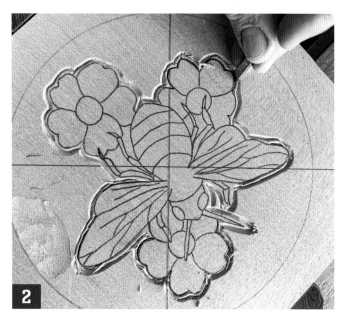

2. Define the bee and flowers. With a 3⁄16" (5mm) 60-degree V-tool, outline the entire scene, using a mallet for control. Then, set in (or vertically cut down around) the image using suitably sized gouges. For the flower petals and wing tips, I used a 3⁄16" (5mm) #5 gouge; for the wings, I used a 5⁄16" (8mm) chisel and a 9⁄16" (14mm) #2 gouge. When it comes to the fragile legs and antennae, give yourself extra space and set in 1⁄32" (1mm) outside the line.

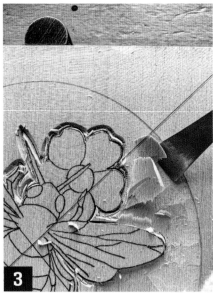
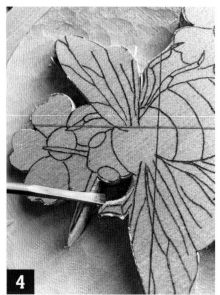
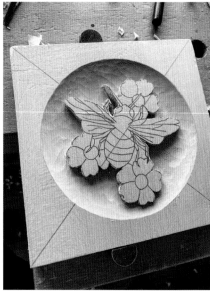

3. Scoop out the inner circle. Position a ¾" (19mm) #3 gouge on the inner line of the circle and carve inward toward the flowers and bee, starting shallow and getting deeper toward the image. Turning the carving around as you go will help here.

4. Refine the circle. So that it's possible to remove wood to a nice depth, you will need to reset in around the image as you go to release the wood. Take this stage slowly, removing thin layers at a time to remove wood in a uniform manner around the circle. Take the depth down until it is between ⅜" and ⁹⁄₁₆" (1 to 1.4cm) by the bee's body; the deeper you go, the more dramatic the relief will be.

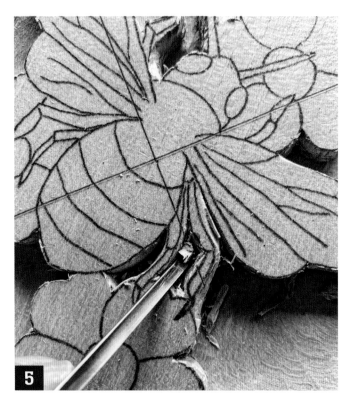

5. Refine the perimeter of the bee. Set in around the legs and bee's body using the smallest gouges you have; I used a ¼" (6mm) #3 and a ⅛" (3mm) #3 gouge, but if you have micro tools, they will come in handy here, as well. Gradually and gently remove the wood until you are level with the rest of the background.

6. Prepare to lower the flowers. With the ³⁄₁₆" (5mm) 60-degree V-tool, outline the antennae, legs, and body of the bee, wherever the bee overlaps with the flowers. Set in these areas using the appropriate tools; I used the ¼" (6mm) #3 gouge, ⅛" (3mm) #3 gouge, and a ¹⁄₃₂" (1mm) micro gouge for the legs, a ⁵⁄₁₆" (8mm) chisel for the antennae, a ⁹⁄₁₆" (14mm) #3 gouge for the body, and the ³⁄₁₆" (5mm) #5 gouge for the head and right eye.

7. Lower the flowers. Using the 9/16" (14mm) #3 gouge, lower the level of the flowers where the bee parts overlap them. Then, level out the surface of the flowers and draw the flower details back in.

8. Define the flower parts. Using a 1/4" (6mm) #7 gouge or similar, set in each flower center. Then, using the 9/16" (14mm) #3 gouge, set in the edges of the petals. With the 5/16" (8mm) #7 gouge, remove wood around the flower centers, and round them over into button shapes using the 1/4" (6mm) #3 gouge.

Tip: Careful Cuts

When setting in around small fragile areas, tilt the top of the gouge away from the image when you make the cut; this lessens the likelihood of damage.

9. Layer the petals. Lower the petals that sit below adjacent petals using the 9/16" (14mm) #3 gouge and the 1/4" (6mm) #3 gouge.

10. Separate the legs from the body. Set in the areas where the legs meet the main body, and lower them so the body appears to overlap them. Use the 1/4" (6mm) #3 gouge. Then, round over the legs using the same tool, tapering them slightly toward the tips. Separate and define the individual parts of the legs. Avoid undercutting, and be mindful of the grain direction.

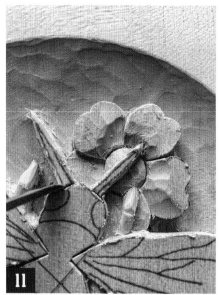

11. Separate the wings and antennae from the body and head. Use the ⁹⁄₁₆" (14mm) #2 gouge or similar. Lower the antennae toward the tips.

12. Rough out the bee body. Round over the body with the ⁹⁄₁₆" (14mm) #3 gouge. Then, use the ³⁄₁₆" (5mm) 60-degree V-tool to separate the head from the body and set in with a gouge of appropriate size. Set in around the eyes with a ³⁄₁₆" (5mm) #6 gouge, and then round them over with the ¼" (6mm) #3 gouge. Round the head and upper segment using the same tool.

13. Rough out the wings. Use the ⁹⁄₁₆" (14mm) #3 gouge to carve over the surface of the wings. Keep the surface flat, as this will be key to giving them a fragile look in later steps. Separate the upper wings from the lower wings with the ³⁄₁₆" (5mm) 60-degree V-tool, set them in with the ⁹⁄₁₆" (14mm) #2 gouge, and then remove wood from the lower wing where it meets the upper to give a sense of overlap.

14. Add the veins and stripes. Redraw the body stripes and wing veins, and then carve over the lines with your ³⁄₁₆" (5mm) 60-degree V-tool, using the mallet for added control. Then, switch over to the petals, scooping out some of the centers with the ⁵⁄₁₆" (8mm) #7 gouge and rounding others down to the background with the ⁹⁄₁₆" (14mm) #3 gouge. You may need to set in the flower centers and petal sides again for easier wood removal. Use your smallest gouge to remove the small pieces of petal that sit under the legs and antennae. Then, add some petal veins with the ³⁄₁₆" (5mm) 60-degree V-tool.

15

Tip: Fragile Feet

It's possible to totally remove the wood from under the back right-hand legs, as the feet are getting support from the flower. However, this is not necessary if you think it is too fragile to carve.

16

15. Undercut the flowers. Use the same tools that you used to set in these areas at the start of the project. For the flowers, take the tool and position it on the sides of a petal, about halfway down from the top surface at an angle of about 40 degrees. Then, cut in, using the mallet, if necessary. Be careful not to cut too deeply or you will mar the background. Continue around the entire shape, and then go around it again, this time holding the gouge flat against the background. Cut in to remove the wood under the flower at the background level.

16. Undercut the wings. Come in at a 45-degree angle, but otherwise follow the same method as in Step 15. I used the ⁹⁄₁₆" (14mm) #3 gouge turned over to help remove wood from the crevices. Then, undercut the legs and the left side of the head. Undercut the antennae only slightly.

17

18

19

17. Clean up. Make sure your gouges are very sharp for this step. Once you are happy with your undercutting, clean up the background with the ⁹⁄₁₆" (14mm) #3 gouge, smoothing it out and removing tool marks. Redefine the flower centers with the ⁵⁄₁₆" (8mm) #7 gouge. Then, with the ¼" (6mm) #3 gouge, tidy up the edges of the entire image. Gently fine-tune the antennae and legs using the ¹⁄₃₂" (1mm) micro gouge.

18. Sand and add texture. With 180-grit sandpaper, gently sand the background and image. Brush off and sand again with 320 grit. ***Note: Make sure to use a mask here to protect your lungs.*** Then, texture the flower centers using a mallet and background punch.

19. Seal the entire carving, including the sides, with beeswax. Rub it in with an old toothbrush and warm it with a hair dryer as you go. Leave for about an hour, and then buff to remove the wax.

Flower Garland in Mahogany

BY LUCY FOX

Flowers are some of my favorite subjects to carve. Whether simple or intricate, they never fail to impress, and the range and type vary enormously. Really, flowers are a fitting focus for both beginners and seasoned carvers. This sweet flower garland is perfect to carve on all those small off-cuts that you don't know how to use but would prefer not to waste. You could leave the panel exactly as is, or repeat it across the surface of a mirror or picture frame.

Tools and Materials

- Mahogany, ¾" (1.9cm) thick: 4" x 12" (10.2 x 30.5cm)
- #3 gouges: ⅛" (3mm), ¼" (6mm), ⁹⁄₁₆" (14mm), ¹³⁄₁₆" (20mm)
- #4 gouge: ⁵⁄₁₆" (8mm)
- #5 gouge: ¼" (6mm)
- #6 gouge: ³⁄₁₆" (5mm)
- #7 gouges: ¼" (6mm), ⁹⁄₁₆" (14mm)
- V-tool: ³⁄₁₆" (5mm) 60-degree
- Pencil
- Mallet
- Clamps or vise
- Graphite transfer paper
- Sandpaper: assorted grits to 320
- Cotton swabs (optional)
- Shellac
- Denatured alcohol
- Dark stain
- Pure beeswax
- Lint-free cloths
- Nail or punch
- Soft brush
- Old toothbrush
- Hair dryer

Getting Started

Drawing the depth line.

Choose a kind of wood. I chose mahogany because the wood holds detail well and has a wonderful luster when finished, but this design would work on many varieties of timber, including basswood, (I recommend gilding for added interest, if you use this variety). Transfer the pattern to the wood blank. I used graphite paper and a pencil. The pattern should be centered on the wood, with the grain running in the same direction as the garland stem. With a pencil, draw a line approximately halfway down the thickness of the piece of wood. This will be your depth guide. Secure the wood with clamps or a vise.

Tips: Before You Carve

- Be careful around the points of the leaves, as they can easily break off.
- Undercut the leaves and petals as you feel comfortable; the more undercut they are, the more delicate they will appear.
- You can remove a good amount of wood in the deepest parts, such as where the petals meet the flower centers and where the petals overlap the leaves.
- For some variation, try rounding over the odd petal instead of scooping it out.
- Use cotton swabs to clean up excess wood stain from hard-to-reach crevices.

Pattern on page 131.

Instructions

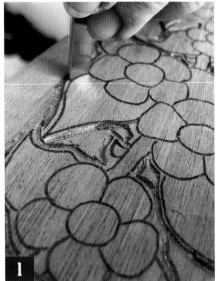

1. Outline the design. Using a ³⁄₁₆" (5mm) 60-degree V-tool, carefully carve around the design just outside the line; you want the line to remain visible. Using a mallet will give you greater control here, as well as lessen the likelihood of slipping. However, this tool is not essential. Once you have gone around the entire design, set in the lines with the best-matching gouges for each area. Make sure to cut directly perpendicular to the surface of the wood; undercutting should be avoided at this stage. Do not go too deep just yet, as it's much safer to increase the depth of your cuts gradually.

2. Remove the waste wood around the design. Using a ⁹⁄₁₆" (14mm) #7 gouge, cut across the grain from the sides up to the design. It's better to use a mallet here. Try to keep the top side edges of the gouge above the wood as you cut across the grain to prevent breakout (removing more wood than intended). Remove the waste wood in stages, taking the surface down to just above the depth line. Repeat the stop cuts along the lines as needed. Once most of the wood is removed, use a ⁹⁄₁₆" (14mm) #3 gouge to achieve a flatter surface. Carefully remove wood from the smaller inner areas and around the stalk and thorns using your smallest gouge; I used a ⅛" (3mm) #3 gouge.

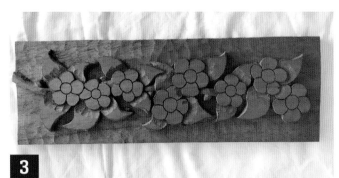

3. Redefine the perimeter. Make sure every leaf and flower is defined fully with a stop cut using the same assortment of gouges as before. Then, begin to add levels. For the petals, I used a ¼" (6mm) #5 gouge and defined the center of the flower with a ³⁄₁₆" (5mm) #6 gouge. The leaves need to look as though they are coming out from behind the flowers, so lower the leaves at these points and in any other areas that need to be lowered to make the design look realistic. I used a ⁵⁄₁₆" (8mm) #4 gouge. The visible stalk areas can be a little tricky to lower, so take it slow and gently round over the edges of the stalk and thorns using the ⅛" (3mm) #3 gouge.

4. Add the leaf veins. Use the ³⁄₁₆" (5mm) 60-degree V-tool. The leaves will look realistic if they are a little different, so decide if you want them to curl up or down, have a central scoop, or dip down on one side. For dramatic curls, make sure to use a gouge with a good curve. Using a ¼" (6mm) #7 gouge and the ⁹⁄₁₆" (14mm) #7 gouge, scoop out wood from the edges of the leaves toward the central vein. Smooth the surfaces of the leaves with a ¼" (6mm) #3 gouge. Here, you can begin to make the carving your own. Try to work with the grain and exaggerate a curl in areas where the grain supports this. In areas where the grain is short, it's best to keep the design shallow or not to touch it at all. Tidy the outside edges of the leaves with the ¼" (6mm) #3 gouge, removing all traces of graphite.

5. Define the flower centers. With the ¼" (6mm) #5 gouge, clear around 1⁄16" (2mm) of wood from around the core of each flower, keeping the height of the center as is. Now round over the center with the ¼" (6mm) #5 gouge, following the grain. You are aiming for a gently rounded, button-like center. Notice that in my version, the petals sit behind or in front of those next to them. Remove a little wood from the lower petals to create this effect. Using the ¼" (6mm) #7 gouge, scoop wood from the centers of the petals. Removing very little, gently smooth over the outside edges of the petals with the ¼" (6mm) #3 gouge. Again, redefine the stop cuts around the perimeter of the design as needed.

6. Add undercutting around the outer edge. I used the ¼" (6mm) #3 gouge, the ¼" (6mm) #5 gouge, and the 9⁄16" (14mm) #3 gouge. Be careful not to dig too hard, as this could mar the smooth background. Tidy any messy areas on the background using a 13⁄16" (20mm) #3 gouge, bringing the background down to the final depth line.

7. Add the finishing touches. With the 3⁄16" (5mm) 60-degree V-tool, reinforce the central vein lines on the leaves, adding secondary veins, if desired. Embellish the flowers by adding lines running from the outside edge of the petal to the center. Using a punch or a small nail, gently pepper the center of each flower with speckles. Clean up your cuts.

8. Sand the piece. I did a light hand-sanding using 150 grit, progressing through the grits until I reached 320.

9. Apply a finish. Using shellac mixed with a little denatured alcohol (at about a 70/30 ratio), coat the surface of the carving two to three times. Lightly sand with 320-grit sandpaper between coats, if necessary. Then, apply a dark stain. With a small brush, rub the stain into the surface of the carving, paying attention to all the small crevices. Once covered, rub the carving with a lint-free cloth and let dry overnight. Then, with an old toothbrush, gently run natural beeswax over the carving and let dry. Once dry, heat the carving from a distance using a hair dryer. Rub off the excess with a lint-free cloth and let dry. Buff with a soft brush and display.

Rosette

BY ROBERT KENNEDY

Rosettes in sculpture have been around since antiquity. They can be found decorating statues, temples, churches, molding, furniture, and even military awards. The design variants are numerous and largely floral in nature, consisting of leaves or petals radiating from a central hub. You can attach the appliqué to any object you prefer, but in this instance, I applied my cherry wood rosette to the top of a keepsake box.

Getting Started

Attach the template to the blank with spray adhesive. Cut out the design using a band saw, scroll saw, or coping saw. Then, prepare your work surface. Thin some wood glue at a ratio of four parts glue to one part water. Brush the glue onto a piece of scrap plywood (this will function as your backing board), place a piece of drawing paper on top, brush the glue on the back of the carving blank, and then place this on top of the paper. Clamp together and allow to dry overnight. This will allow you to clamp the backing board to your work surface and carve the rosette freely. Drill the holes for the eyelets; I used a $^{11}\!/_{64}$" (4.4mm)-dia. bit for the inner eyelets and a $^5\!/_{32}$" (4mm)-dia. bit for the outer ones.

Tools and Materials

- Cherry, $^5\!/_8$" (1.6cm) thick: $4\frac{1}{2}$" (11.4cm) square
- Scrap plywood (for backing board)
- Carving knife
- Putty knife
- #3 gouge: $^3\!/_8$" (10mm)
- #6 gouges: $^1\!/_8$" (3mm), $^1\!/_4$" (6mm), $^5\!/_{16}$" (8mm)
- #8 gouges: $^3\!/_8$" (10mm), $^3\!/_4$" (19mm)
- #9 gouge: $^1\!/_8$" (3mm)
- #11 gouges: $^1\!/_8$" (3mm), $^1\!/_4$" (6mm)
- V-tool: $^1\!/_{16}$" (2mm) 45-degree
- Skew chisel: $^3\!/_8$" (10mm)
- Band saw, coping saw, or scroll saw
- Marking gauge
- Drill with bits: $^5\!/_{32}$" (4mm), $^{11}\!/_{64}$" (4.4mm)
- Sandpaper: 100 grit
- Medium-weight drawing paper: 1 sheet
- Spray adhesive
- Wax-based pencils
- Wood glue
- Boiled linseed oil
- Mineral spirits
- Paintbrushes: disposable foam (for applying finish)
- Clear paste wax
- Clean cloth
- Masking tape
- Clamps
- Marker

Tip: Make a Marking Gauge

If you don't own a marking gauge, you can make a simple one with a wood screw and a small piece of wood. Simply sharpen the head of the screw using a bench stone or rotary tool with a stone bit. Predrill a hole the size of the screw, and adjust depth with a screwdriver.

Pattern on pages 136–38.

Instructions

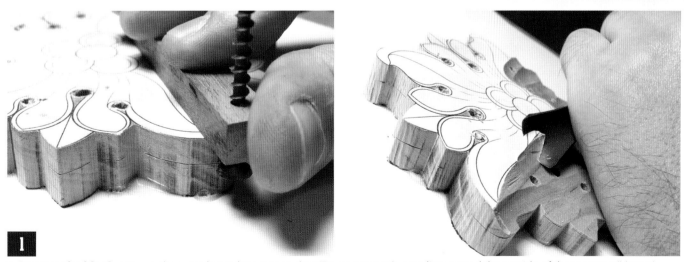

1

1. Prepare the blank. Using a shop-made marking gauge, (see Tip on page 66), cut a line around the outside of the rosette ¼" (6mm) down from the surface. Then, begin removing material from the outside of the inner petals down to the line you just marked, leaving the central flower intact. Use a ¾" (19mm) #8 gouge.

2. Rough in the central flower. Using a ¼" (6mm) #11 gouge, carve the outline of the inner petals, cutting close to the line but not touching it. Then, use a ⁵⁄₁₆" (8mm) #6 gouge to create a ¼" (6mm)-deep stop cut all the way around the inner petals.

3. Refine the central flower. Use the ⁵⁄₁₆" (8mm) #6 gouge to create a ⅛" (3mm)-deep stop cut, continuing the inner petal line to the center circle. Outline the center circle with a ¼" (6mm) #6 gouge, making stop cuts ⅛" (3mm) deep.

4. Mark the body of the rosette. With the template mostly carved away, draw the features of the rosette directly on the wood. I also number the sections according to depth, #1 being the highest point to #4 being the lowest point. I used a fine-point permanent marker for the sake of visibility in these photos, but I tend to use wax-based pencils, as the graphite variety can smear.

5. Begin rounding the inner petals. Use a ⅜" (10mm) #3 gouge. I cut at a slight angle down to the sidewall of the petal before rounding (the arrows indicate high to low relief). Then, cut a slightly rounded bevel ⅛" (3mm) wide around the circumference of the petal using the concave side of the gouge. You can carve the inner petals all at once, but I prefer to cut them as I move to each section of the greater carving.

6. Mark the high points. These will look like tubes radiating out from the central flower. Then, using a ⅛" (3mm) #9 gouge, cut a ³⁄₁₆" (5mm)-deep channel on either side of each tube, cutting toward the inner petals. Cut a channel along the inner edge of the major petal. Then, carve the surrounding areas of the major petal down to the channel depth using the ¼" (6mm) #6 gouge. Cut the centerline of the major petal; use a ¹⁄₁₆" (2mm) 45-degree V-tool.

7. Refine the inner edge of the major petal. Use the ⁵⁄₁₆" (8mm) #6 gouge. Make slicing cuts, angling the handle slightly toward yourself so the corner furthest from you is slightly raised. This prevents it from marring the surface of the work. Push forward gently with your thumb, using your other hand on the handle to control the cutting radius. Take care to keep your fingers away from the cutting path. Stop the cut right before the eyelet. Then, reinforce the centerline of the major petal, following the groove previously made with the V-tool. Use a carving knife.

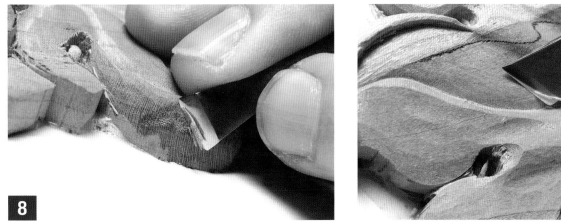

8. Round the outside edge of the major petal. Use the concave side of a ³⁄₈" (10mm) #8 gouge. Then, use a ³⁄₈" (10mm) skew chisel to contour the major petal down to its centerline. I also use the skew chisel to round over the left side of the major petal, from the eyelet to the inner edge.

9. Continue rounding over the major petals. Use the ³⁄₈" (10mm) skew chisel to gently contour the tubes without erasing any of the details you already created. Switch to a ⅛" (3mm) #11 gouge to smooth out the point between the convex and concave sides of the tubes. This will create a rippling effect on the surface.

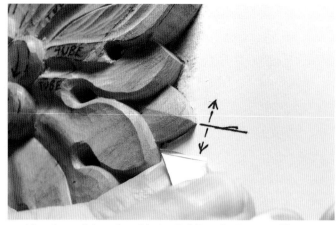

10. Rough in the tabs (around the exterior). Make a stop cut on the outside edges of the tabs with the ⁵⁄₁₆" (8mm) #6 gouge. Then, lower the surface of each one with the ⅜" (10mm) skew chisel until the tab sits ³⁄₁₆" (5mm) up from the backing board. Draw a centerline from where the two minor petals join with the tip of the tab, and then use the ⅜" (10mm) skew chisel to bevel each side of the tab. This gives it a spear-like look. *Note: The flat sides of the tab should now be ¹⁄₁₆" (2mm) high.*

11. Shape the minor petals. These will be around the same height as the major petals, with a slight concave shape. Use the ⅜" (10mm) #3 gouge.

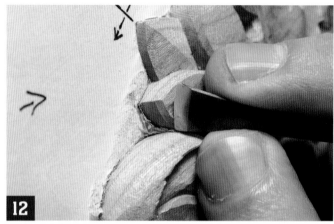

12. Bevel the edges of the minor petals. Using the concave side of the ⅜" (10mm) #3 gouge, cut a ¹⁄₁₆" (2mm)-wide bevel around the perimeter of the minor petals. Then, cut a very small bevel on the inner edge of the major petal, ⅜" (1cm) wide at most.

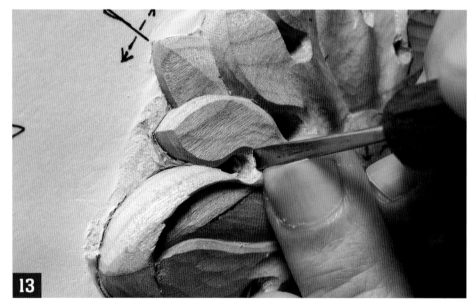

13. Continue the bevel into the eyelets. Use a ⅛" (3mm) #6 gouge. All five main "spokes" of the rosette are the same, so use the previous steps to continue around the radius of the rosette (if you haven't already), cutting with the grain as cleanly as possible. For the outside sidewalls, use the ⅜" (10mm) skew chisel, ⅜" (10mm) #3 gouge, and ⅛" (3mm) #6 gouge. Make sure these are very sharp, as you'll be cleanly cutting end grain. *Note: My technique for this is to use downward slicing cuts, making very thin shavings and stropping the chisel if I notice any tearing in the end grain.*

14. Shape the inner flower. Use the ¼" (6mm) #6 gouge to cut a concave depression in each, starting from the inside bevel and continuing to the center stop cut.

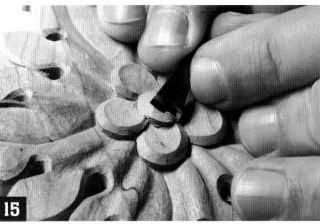

15. Round the center. Use the concave side of the ⅜" (10mm) #3 gouge, taking a little off at a time. Round all the way to its junction with the center petals. Then, look over the entire carving, keeping an eye out for loose fibers or torn grain, and clean up those areas as needed.

16. Free the carving from the backing board. Use a very thin putty knife, pushing in toward the center. Do this slowly, working around the radius a little at a time. If done right, the carving should pop free with little to no prying. Be especially careful around the tabs, as they are the thinnest part of the rosette. Lay a sheet of 100-grit sandpaper on a flat work surface, and sand the residual glue and paper off the back of the rosette, using circular motions. If the insides of the eyelets are a bit rough, cut a small section of the sandpaper and work it through those areas to sand them smooth. Once done, apply your finish of choice.

Finishing

I do not sand the carved surface of the rosette, as I prefer a natural, chiseled finish. Before you finish the rosette, apply a thin coat of wood glue to the back of the carving and attach it to the top of the box. Note: Make sure it is centered. To avoid damaging the carving with clamps, I use masking tape—three strips horizontal and three strips vertical—to hold it in place. Let the assembly dry overnight.

Finish the box. With the glue dry, I brush a mixture of two parts mineral spirits to one part boiled linseed oil all over the carving and the outside of the box. Wait 15 minutes and wipe off the excess with a clean cloth. Leave it to dry at least 24 hours and follow with two coats of plain boiled linseed oil applied in the same way. (The mineral spirits just help the first coat absorb into the wood.) Finally, apply a thin coat of clear paste wax to the entire carving and box, inside and out. After 15 minutes, buff with a clean cloth until the project shines. Apply one or two more coats, using the same technique, and then leave the box untouched for 24 hours.

Celtic Knotwork

BY LISA LAUGHY

I originally designed this pattern as a wedding gift, but it is also a wonderful project to make as an anniversary gift or for Valentine's Day; your love will show in the time and care you put into creating it. Carving Celtic knots can be challenging, as it takes a careful eye to create the illusion of the over-and-under flow of strands that make up the knots. This project is a great way to get started. The simplified design, once completed, will give you the confidence to take on larger, more complex knotwork patterns in the future.

Tools and Materials

- Mahogany, ⅞" (2.2cm) thick: 6½" x 11⅞" (16.5 x 30.2cm)
- Carving knife
- #1 skew chisel: ½" (13mm) double bevel
- #2 gouges: ½" (13mm), 1³⁄₁₆" (30mm)
- #3 gouges: 1" (25mm) fishtail, 1³⁄₁₆" (30mm)
- #5 gouges: ¹³⁄₃₂" (10mm), 1" (25mm) fishtail
- #8 gouges: ⁹⁄₃₂" (7mm), 1³⁄₆₄" (5mm)
- #20 gouge: ²⁵⁄₃₂" (20mm) back-bent (optional)
- #25 gouge: ½" (13mm) back-bent (optional)
- V-tool: ¹⁵⁄₃₂" (12mm) 35-degree
- Band saw, scroll saw, coping saw, or jig saw
- Drill or drill press with bits: ⁵⁄₃₂" (4mm), ¹¹⁄₁₆" (4.4mm)
- Gimlet auger

- Mallet
- Scissors or hobby knife
- Toothbrush
- Shoe brush
- Chip brush
- Files: 4 ¹¹⁄₃₂" (110mm) half-round extreme-fine cut, 4 ¹¹⁄₃₂" (110mm) flat extra-fine cut, 7⅞" (200mm) flat extreme-fine cut
- Spindle sander
- Pencil
- Masking tape
- Odorless mineral spirits
- Boiled linseed oil
- Medium wax finish
- Clean, dry rags
- Hanger of choice
- Clamps
- Router or CNC machine (optional)
- Spray adhesive
- Wood glue

Getting Started

Attach the template to the blank with spray adhesive. Cut out the design using a band saw, scroll saw, or coping saw. Then, prepare your work surface. Thin some wood glue at a ratio of four parts glue to one part water. Brush the glue onto a piece of scrap plywood (this will function as your backing board), place a piece of drawing paper on top, brush the glue on the back of the carving blank, and then place this on top of the paper. Clamp together and allow to dry overnight. This will allow you to clamp the backing board to your work surface and carve the rosette freely. Drill the holes for the eyelets; I used a ¹¹⁄₆₄" (4.4mm)-dia. bit for the inner eyelets and a ⁵⁄₃₂" (4mm)-dia. bit for the outer ones.

Choose your wood and check for defects.

Enlarge the pattern to the size you want your carving to be. Carefully cut out your pattern and secure it to the wood with masking tape. With a pencil, draw around the outline and inner holes onto the wood. Remove the pattern and draw the lines for the knotwork strands. Drill the interior holes and make the interior cuts with a scroll saw. Then, cut the shape using a band saw, scroll saw, or jig saw. *Note: You can also use a router to remove the interior holes, or cut the whole pattern using a CNC machine.*

Apply the pattern.

Pattern on page 138.

Instructions

1. File the edges. Use wood files on the edges to get the shape as close to the pattern lines as possible. You can also use a combination of a spindle sander and then files to reach the areas the spindle can't reach. Once the edges are filed, make a pencil line around the interior and exterior edges, marking half the thickness of your piece. You will use this pencil line as a guide for rounding the edges in Step 4.

2. Make stop cuts. Using a mallet and a large 1³⁄₁₆" (30mm) #3 gouge, establish the stop cuts at the junctions of the strands. Then, use a ¹⁵⁄₃₂" (12mm) 35-degree V-tool to cut down on the lower side of the junction, keeping the edge of the cut at a 90-degree angle.

3. Add terraces. Using a ¹³⁄₆₄" (10mm) #8 gouge, create terraced grooves, with the deepest point at the junction halfway to the pencil line—roughly ¼ of the wood's thickness. Create terraces at each junction, keeping the depth and manner of descent consistent throughout the whole piece.

4. Round the outside edges. With a 1" (25mm) #5 gouge held upside down, round the outside edges, using the pencil line as a guide. Use the gouge right-side up on the inner curves of the strands. Refine this rounding using a 1" (25mm) #3 gouge. Fishtail gouges work best for both of these steps, but use what you have on hand. Use a 1 ³⁄₁₆" (30mm) #2 gouge to refine the rounding, particularly on the top of the strand.

5. Round the inside edges. Using a ½" (13mm) #1 double-bevel skew chisel, round the inside edges down to the pencil line. This can also be done with a fine-tipped carving knife, such as the Morakniv 106. Clean the bottom half of the inside edge, as well as the flat section—it is sometimes easier to access this from the back of the carving.

6. Refine your work. Go over the entire carving, taking down any remaining ridges from earlier steps. Use an assortment of tools to make smaller and finer cuts, leaving a nice, clean, slightly rippled surface. Clean up the inside and outside edges using the carving knife.

7. Prepare the piece for hardware. Measure and mark a centerline on the back of the carving. Mark the holes to attach a hanger; the screw needs to be short enough to avoid breaking through the front. Make a pilot hole for the screw and carve a recess so that it will hang flush to the wall. Carve your signature on the back of the carving. Wait to attach hardware until finished is applied.

Tip: Textured Finish

I finish all my carvings from the tool, which means I never sand them. This way of carving takes more time to refine the work, but the results are well worth it. Each mark of the tool shows in the work, and creates a subtlety ripped texture to the carving, allowing the light to travel over the surface in a visually pleasing way.

Finishing

Seal your carving with your preferred oil and wax finish. I use an 80/20 mix of boiled linseed oil and odorless mineral spirits. Apply the oil mixture using a small brush, making sure to cover the entire carving, front and back. Allow the oil to soak in for 15 minutes, and then remove excess with a clean rag. Let the carving dry for one to two weeks, until the surface no longer feels oily to the touch.

Apply a light coat of wax to the entire carving using a rag or a toothbrush. I use a beeswax product called Cold Wax Medium, made by Gamblin. Use a clean rag to carefully remove all the excess wax, especially at the junctions. Buff the carving with a clean brush; a new shoe brush works great for this. Continue buffing the carving a few more times over the next couple of days as the wax dries. Attach hanging hardware and your carving is complete!

Apply the finish of your choice and seal the carving.

Use a toothbrush to apply wax to the carving.

Back-Bent Gouges

Back-bent gouges are a nice addition to have in your carving tool collection, particularly if you enjoy carving Celtic knotwork. Their specialized design makes it easier to round the edges and create nicely formed curves.

Botanical Woodland Print

BY BETH LEWIS

Woodcut printmaking is a simple, beautiful, and incredibly fun form of printmaking in which you relieve material around a raised design, roll the design with ink, and then transfer it onto paper. There's nothing quite like the moment when you reveal your first print from a brand-new block. This design will give you the foundation you need to create your own original pieces to display, sell, or give as gifts.

Getting Started

Choose a kind of wood. I chose smooth, strong Shina plywood. It carves like butter and holds details well, so even the tiniest of marks will transfer to your final print.

Sharpen your tools. Your tools will need to be razor-sharp to carve tiny details and keep clean, crisp edges for your print. Use a leather strop and a honing compound.

Cut the wood to size and stain with a watered down, water-based stain or watercolor paint. A light wash in a light color works best; you only want to stain the very top layer of wood, so you can easily see what you are carving away. Allow to air-dry. Then, photocopy the template onto a very thin piece of A4 paper. Lay the pattern face-down on the plywood and transfer the design using graphite paper and a pencil. *Note: The design will be backward on your block, so that later, when you print it, it will be the right way around again.* For the step photos, I placed this image so the grain runs horizontally across the design.

Tools and Materials

- Japanese Shina plywood, ¼" (6mm) thick: 8¼" x 11 ¹¹⁄₁₆" (21 x 29.7cm)
- Palette knife
- #8 U-gouge: ¼" (6mm)
- Micro V-tool: ¹⁄₁₆" (2mm)
- V-tool: ³⁄₁₆" (5mm) 60-degree
- Glass cutting board
- Brayer, 4" (10.2cm)
- Wooden spoon
- Pencil
- Graphite paper
- A4 cartridge paper
- Masking tape
- Stain or acrylic paint
- Water-soluble printmaking ink
- Brush cleaner
- Wiping compound (tack reducer) (optional)
- Baby wipes
- Scrap paper
- Printmaking paper

Instructions

1. Carve the simple leaf outlines and veins. With a ¹⁄₁₆" (2mm) micro V-tool, carve along the leaf edges, starting at corners and working in slow, sweeping motions. Then, carve away the vein lines inside the leaves, starting at the tip of the vein and working your way into the center so the finer end of your line is at the tip of each vein. You'll need to spin and move your block frequently in order to always be cutting away from your body.

2. Carve the toothed leaf margins. Leaves with a jagged, toothed edge (like the rowan leaf) require a bit of patience and practice. Carve a fine line following the highest point of the teeth. Then, holding the ¹⁄₁₆" (2mm) micro V-tool at a steep angle, notch directly down, removing a small triangle of wood. Repeat this technique along all edges.

Pattern on
page 139.

3. Define the fronds. To clear tiny gaps between spaces in fronds (as with the umbrella palm), approach from two angles, carving away from tight corners into the middle, and then spinning the block and carving from the opposite side to meet the cut in the middle. Then, carve the needles, as on the Norway spruce, starting at the center and working outward.

4. Carve the letters. When carving corners on letters like *L*, it's best to start in the outside corner carving outward, extending further than the end of the letter. You can then repeat on the inside corner and finish by notching across the ends of the letter. For letters with sharp edges, such as *M, N,* and *Z,* tackle the inside corners first. Keeping a steep angle to your tool, carefully follow down one edge, returning to the corner and carving down the next edge.

5. Outline the fine details. Switch to a 3⁄16" (5mm) 60-degree V-tool to enlarge and outline the small details you've created. Slowly follow the lines you made with the larger tool, expanding the width of the line into the blank areas. Make not to sure remove any parts of the design you want to leave behind.

6. Clear the islands of wood between leaves. Now that you've expanded your outlines, you'll be left with little islands of wood between leaves and letters. Using a ¼" (6mm) #8 U-gouge, carefully clear these areas, carving with the grain, from one edge to the other.

7. Clear the edges. Using the same tool, start at the edge of the design, carving out with the grain toward the edge of the wood. On the bottom and top of the design, I recommend carving the area away in four or five sections to avoid splitting away larger chips than you intended.

8. Inspect your finished design. Now that you've carved all the details and removed all edges and islands, it's time to inspect each element, making sure you haven't missed anything. Clean up your cuts as necessary and make any final tweaks.

9. Prepare the printing area. Clear away any woodchips, dust, and debris from your space. You will need a wipe-clean area or table. Then, prepare your ink. I use Caligo Safewash, an eco-friendly vegetable oil-based ink that cleans up with soap and water (most oil-based inks use solvents). Squeeze a little ink onto a glass cutting board, mixing with a small amount of tack-reducing compound, if desired. (This helps it print a little easier but isn't essential.) Mix well with a palette knife.

10. Roll out the ink. I use a 4" (10.2cm) brayer. Dip the brayer into a little drop of ink and roll the ink over a roughly 5" by 7" (12.7 by 17.8cm) space, rolling until you have a fine, smooth layer of ink on the glass. The ink should almost make a hissing sound when it's ready.

11. Apply the ink to the block. Now roll your brayer over the surface of the block, taking care not to apply ink to the edges accidentally. Roll in all directions, applying one or two fine layers of ink. *Note: The first few layers soak into the wood slightly, so it usually takes a few prints to find the perfect amount of ink.*

12. Check for high points. On the edges and spaces between leaves, you may find some high points that catch a little ink; make sure to carve these away before you print. Now reapply the ink and wash your hands before printing.

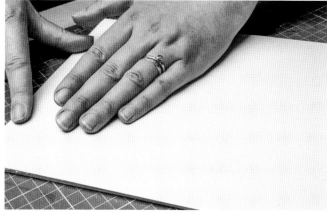

13. Line up the paper. Carefully line up the corners of the wood with the corners of the paper along the short edge. When you're happy with the alignment, slowly let the paper fall onto the inked surface. Then, smooth the paper down. With one hand still holding the paper in place, gently press it onto the surface with the palm of your hand. The sticky ink will hold the paper in place, but it's best to keep your other hand firm on the page, so you don't move the paper and get a smudgy print.

14. Burnish your print. Using the back of a standard wooden spoon, apply a little pressure with three fingers. Then, with gentle, circular motions, rub all over the back of the print, using the other hand to make sure the paper holds still. As you continue, you can add a little more pressure and speed until you begin to see the ink transferring onto the paper. If necessary, take a peek by carefully peeling back a part of the print to see if the ink has transferred well, returning it carefully if it needs more work.

16. Inspect and repeat. Have a good look at your print: are there any blotchy bits or missing ink, smudges, or missed carving? It takes time to perfect this part of the process, so practice with cheap paper and keep tweaking your carving and print attempts until you find one you're satisfied with.

15. Peel and reveal. Once you're happy with your burnishing, gently peel the paper back off the block and admire the perfect symmetry of print and block.

Finishing

Dry your print. Leave your print somewhere safe and dry and allow it to air-dry. Be patient; oil-based inks can take up to a week (or more in winter) to dry! If your prints are taking too long to dry, you might want to adjust how much ink you are using. Frame and enjoy your print, and don't forget to make copies for friends and family! You can experiment with color, types of paper, and lots more as your new hobby progresses.

Clean up. Your tools and table can be easily cleaned with baby wipes or a soapy cloth. If you'd like to keep printing for decades using the same wood block, then it's best to gently wash the surface with a very soft brush and soapy water, drying carefully in a cool, non-humid place. This removes ink properly from all the little gouge marks and maintains the details. If you'd rather keep it as a decorative object, then make a few additional prints from the block without applying more ink. This will slowly remove excess without getting remaining ink onto the carved area.

Pattern on
page 140.

Sunken Greenman

BY LORA S. IRISH

For this project, the background wood—the wood outside the pattern—is left at the original level of the wood surface. Only the actual design area is carved, creating the appearance in the final carving that the face is sunken into the wood. This low-relief carving does not include any undercutting.

Throughout this tutorial, I'll be referring to the tools in a semi-generic way. The actual sweep and size of the tools is less important than the overall action of the cut. I've cited suggested gouge sweeps and sizes in the materials list, but any tool you have that is close to those sizes and sweeps will work.

I use a thick terrycloth towel or nonslip mat to hold the blank in place while I carve.

Tools and Materials

- Basswood, ¾" (19mm) thick: 9" x 12" (22.9 x 30.5cm)
- Bench knife
- Large and small round gouges, such as a ⅜" (10mm) #8 and ⅛" (3mm) #8
- Straight chisel: ⅜" (10mm) wide
- Wide sweep round gouge, such as a ½" (13mm) #3 gouge
- V-gouge or V-tool: ¼" (6mm) 90-degree
- Bull-nose chisel: ⅜" (10mm) wide
- Pencil
- Fine-point permanent marker
- Ruler
- Sandpaper: 220-grit
- Graphite paper
- Sanding sealer
- Polyurethane spray sealer
- Pecan oil stain
- Thick terrycloth towel or nonslip mat
- Soft, clean cloth

Instructions

1. Transfer the pattern and cut the outlines. Prepare the board by lightly sanding it with 220-grit sandpaper. Remove the sanding dust with a dry, clean cloth. Use graphite paper to trace the pattern onto the blank. Using a pencil and ruler, measure and mark a border ½" (13mm) from the edges on all four sides of the blank. Measure and mark a second border ¾" (19mm) from the edges on all four sides. With a V-gouge, carve along the outer pattern lines of the face and along both border lines. With a straight chisel, bevel the sides of the border line cuts.

2. Cut and shape the background leaves. Use a bench knife to make stop cuts along the pattern lines of the lowest leaf clusters around the mouth and mustache (Level 1). With a large and/or small round gouge, rough cut the background leaves (Level 4), tapering them from their highest point at the outer edge of the pattern to their lowest point where they intersect with the face and upper leaf clusters.

3. Refine the leaves. Smooth the background leaves, and shape the mouth leaves. Use a wide-sweep gouge or large round gouge to remove the tool marks left from carving the background leaves. With the bench knife, make stop cuts along the leaves extending from the mouth and then round the edges. With a V-gouge, carve a groove in the center of each leaf to simulate a vein. Round the lips with a straight chisel.

4. Shape the eyeballs. Use a V-gouge to make cuts around the upper and lower eyelids. Use a straight chisel or wide-sweep round gouge to round the eyeballs. Shape the upper eyebrow area with a straight chisel or a wide sweep gouge.

5. Shape the face. Cut with the V-gouge from the corner of each eye to the side of the face. Round the edges of the face with a straight chisel. Round and shape the area above and below the eyelids (Level 3) with a straight chisel.

6. Carve the pupils. Upend a large round gouge, and cut the outline of a three-quarter circle at the top of each eye. Free the circular chips with a bench knife. The indented circles represent the pupils of the eyes.

7. Shape the cheeks and nostrils. Cut along the sides of the nose with a V-gouge. Shape the sides of the face next to the nose (Level 3) with a straight chisel or a wide sweep gouge. Upend a small round gouge and cut the outline of a three-quarter circle for each nostril. Remove the nostril chips with a bench knife.

8. Add the facial details. Taper the nose to its lowest point at the bridge with a straight chisel. With a V-gouge, cut wrinkle lines at the corner of the eyes, under the eyes, and from the corner of the nostrils into the lower cheek area. Finish shaping the mustache leaves, eyebrow leaves, and the leaves at the top of the nose.

9. Carve the background details. Use a pencil to mark the detail leaf lines into the lower section of the facial leaves. Make stop cuts along the pencil lines using a V-gouge. With a straight chisel, bevel one side of each leaf to tuck it under the leaf above it.

Finishing

Smooth the carving by shaving the carved areas with a wide-sweep gouge, bull-nose chisel, or straight chisel. Lightly sand the carving using 220-grit sandpaper, and remove the dust with a dry, clean cloth. Spray two coats of sanding sealer over the entire carving, following the manufacturer's instructions. Sand after each coat. Sign and date the back of the carving with a fine-point permanent marker.

Following the manufacturer's instructions, apply one coat of pecan oil stain to the carving. Apply the stain to an area about 3" (7.6cm) square, and then wipe the carving with a dry, clean cloth. Allow the stain to dry completely. Seal the work with two light coats of polyurethane spray sealer.

Fall Scene in Low Relief

BY FRED AND ELAINE STENMAN

Our low-relief style of carving is really a matter of using three different skills in concert. We start with a layer of carving—only some elements are carved. Then, we add details with a woodburner and finish with a layer of transparent painting. The resulting scene has so much color and dimension that you'll want to jump right in and start hauling pumpkins to the barn yourself. Once you've completed this project, apply our technique to any scene that strikes your fancy; the world is yours to capture.

Tools and Materials

- Basswood, 1" (2.5cm) thick: 12½" (31.8cm) semi round with bark on the bottom
- Stop board (optional)
- Bent chip-carving knife
- #3 gouges: assorted sizes from ⅜" (10mm) to 1⅜" (35mm)
- #11 veiner: ¹⁄₁₆" (2mm)
- Drill with Sand-O-Flex Sander: 150 grit
- Woodburner with nibs: skew; tight round
- Thick rubber shelf mats (2)
- Pencil
- Graphite paper
- Abranet sanding mesh
- Acrylic paints: antique gold, black, burnt sienna, burnt umber, charcoal grey, dark burnt umber, dark forest green, forest green, heritage brick, hippo grey, pumpkin, raw sienna, tangerine, titanium white, trail tan, true red
- Paint thinner: solvent based, such as mineral spirits
- Oil paint: burnt umber
- Paintbrushes: ⅜" (10mm) angled shader, ½" (13mm) angled shader, 2/0 short liner, stiff ¾" (19mm) to scrub oil paint; 1" (25mm) to paint edge
- Finish, such as wipe-on polyurethane
- Polishing pad
- Brown paper bag

Tip: Safe Carving

For projects like this, always place the blank on top of a nonslip rubber mat (such as a shelf liner). This keeps the carving from moving while you work. Keep both hands on the knife or gouge (to keep your skin away from the sharp edge) or wear a carving glove.

Instructions

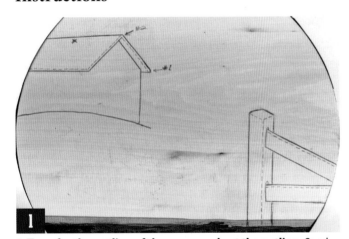

1. Transfer the outline of the scene and cut the outline. Sand it smooth. Tape the pattern in place and slip graphite paper under the pattern. Make sure the building wall is perpendicular to the bottom of the blank. Trace the outline of the building and fence (marked in red on the pattern) with a ballpoint pen. *Note: Arrow #1 shows where the roof goes behind the wall. The end of the fascia board is square to the wall. Arrow #2 shows that the stop cut does not go the whole way to the peak.* Make a copy of the pattern and cut out the building and fence. The pattern will lie down on the board and can be more easily traced with graphite prior to Step 10.

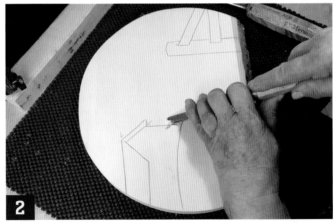

2. Make stop cuts along the lines. With a thin-bladed, bent chip-carving knife, make the cuts about ⅛" (3mm) deep and perpendicular to the surface of the wood. Deepen all the cuts except the rooflines to ¼" (6mm). Remove ⅛" (3mm) of the background with a series of #3 gouges ranging from ⅜" (10mm) wide to 1⅜" (35mm) wide. Do not remove any wood below the building; the background is shallow at the bottom and goes deeper (¼" or 6mm) as you go up. Round the top of the slot above each rail with a ¹⁄₁₆" (2mm) veiner.

Pattern on page 141.

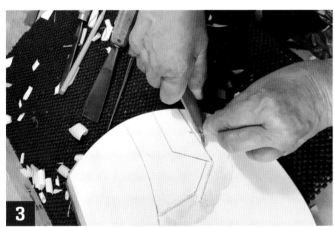

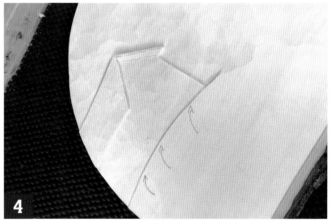

3. Undercut the eave. Insert the knife at a 45-degree angle behind the eave at the new lowered plane. Make a stop cut from the bottom to the peak. Make a similar stop cut at a 45-degree angle along the roofline starting at the peak. Draw the knife back along the roofline to the X. Then, rotate the knife 90 degrees to make the rest of the cut. This method allows you to undercut only the right half of the roofline. Remove and smooth the background with the 1⅜" (35mm) #3 gouge. The depth of the edge of the roof is the same from left to right.

4. Carve down the front and left side walls. Remove about ⅛" (3mm) of their thickness. Leave the roof, eaves, and the ground below the building at the full thickness of the board and protruding above the walls. Because this is a very shallow relief, do not bend the wall at the corner of the building. The front and left sidewall are relieved back on the same plane. Later, we will shade the leftmost side with darker paint.

Intermediate Projects: Fall Scene in Low Relief   **85**

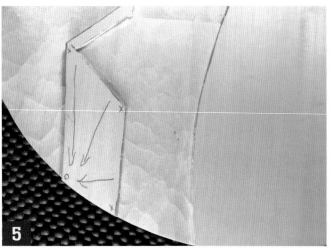
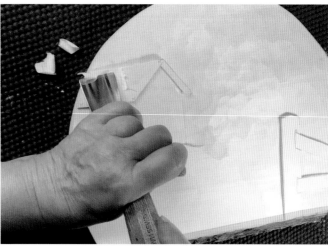

5. Carve the roof at an angle. Work from the three marked Xs on the roof to the O on the left upper corner of the roof, which is carved almost down to the background. This new plane can be flat, but will be even more effective if it is slightly concave.

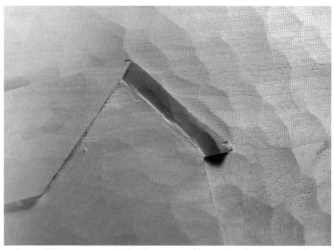

6. Carve the gable eave at an angle to the wall. The eave should meet the wall like a paper fold. The arrows show the direction of the cuts. Do not allow the edge of the shallow gouge to cut into the wall. The bottom arrow on the eave reminds you to tuck the eave behind the wall.

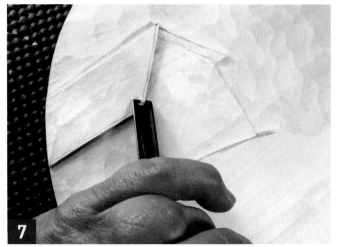

7. Draw a line along the inside of the fascia boards. Create a new plane by angling the shallow gouge slightly and follow the line. Do not angle the fascia board under the wall. Carve up along the left gable to create the fascia board and down the right side to avoid any tear out. Undercut the rooftop and gable side using the knife or the shallow gouge. Do not pry it out. Carve as cleanly as possible in this area.

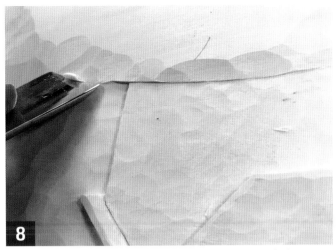

8. Round the ground down to the building. Carve a light texture in the foreground area. The cuts should vary in size; do not carve them in rows. Keep the corner of your gouge from cutting into the building wall.

Clean Up Spots

Before adding the burned texture, clean up any rough carved spots. Then, hand-sand the board with 120-grit Abranet. Use a 150-grit Sand-O-Flex sander in a drill to smooth the final surface. Draw or trace the full pattern onto the blank.

9. Leave the fence post square. Carve the left side (the front) lightly, but keep it flat; do not angle it toward the background. Angle the right side strongly back to the background. Taper the top of the post to the background. Carve about half the thickness off the fence rails. Keep them flat to the surface. Tuck the end of the rails into the slot on the post. Draw a line 1/16" (2mm) down from the top of both rails. Taper the top of each rail back toward the background to create the thickness of the rail.

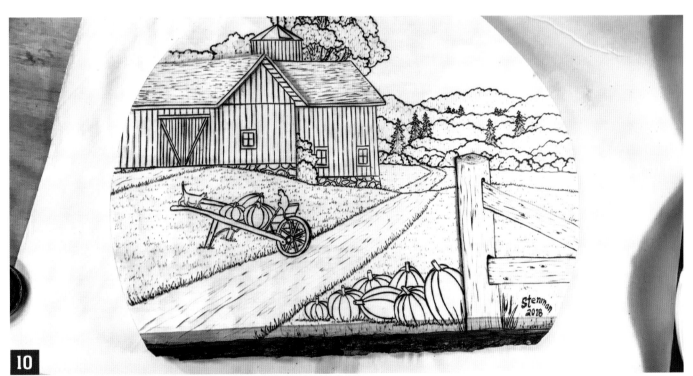

10. Woodburn along all the carved lines and around the details. Use a skew nib, such as a Colwood B or Optima PH 11, for the straight lines. Use the edge of a tight round nib, such as a Colwood J (slightly bent to a spoon shape), for the curved lines. The outside lines are strongly burned, dark, and continuous. This is necessary to keep the thinned paint inside the burn line. Burn light texture into most areas to break up but not fill up the wood grain. Make soft curvy squiggles for the tree and shrub texture. Add texture to the large grass areas and include patches of different lengths and heights. Burn darker grass lines on the edge of a road or path to define the edge. Be sure to burn your signature on your carving.

Where to Paint

Paint directly onto the raw wood. Do not apply a sealer. Thin the acrylic paint heavily with water. For this project, we use an earth tone color palette. Avoid bright, gaudy colors.

11. Paint the grass. Mix dark forest green and burnt umber and thin it heavily with water. Add streaks of thinned antique gold and thinned burnt sienna, and smudge them into the still wet green paint to soften the streaks.

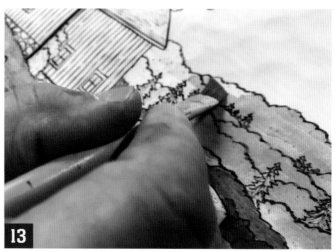

12. Paint the red on the shrubs. Use thinned heritage brick. Shade the bottoms of the shrubs with a dark green and stipple with thicker heritage brick to brighten them. Paint the green shrubs dark forest green mixed with a small amount of burnt umber thinned heavily with water. Add color by stippling these shrubs with antique gold, tangerine, and heritage brick.

13. Paint the top foliage sections with thinned antique gold. Stipple these areas with unthinned tangerine and heritage brick. Dry-brush the bottoms of all the wet gold sections with forest green (not dark forest green) to add shadows.

14. Paint the tree canopy behind the roof. Use thinned burnt sienna. While the paint is still wet, dry-brush the bottoms of each section with true red and blend lightly. Paint the trunk and limbs with thinned dark burnt umber. Paint the evergreen trees with a medium thick coat of green created by mixing dark forest green, some black, and some burnt umber thinned slightly with water.

15. Paint the non-shadowed walls with thinned white and the shadowed side with thinned white plus a bit of hippo grey. Use this gray mix for the eave's shadow, too. Re-burn the siding boards as needed. Apply thin heritage brick to the front shrubs, shading and stippling them as demonstrated in Step 12. Paint the windows dark burnt umber. Coat the silo and top with very thin hippo grey, highlight the right side with very thin white, and shade the left with very thin charcoal. Color the open slot dark burnt umber. Paint the road with a thin raw sienna mix, adding burnt umber and hippo grey, and smudge the edges and ruts while wet. For the foundation, use thin trail tan and dry-brush burnt umber and hippo grey on stones. Finish the roof with unthinned dark forest green.

17. Paint the pumpkins with thinned pumpkin (orange). While still wet, dry-brush the left sides of the pumpkins with burnt sienna to shade. Dry-brush the right sides with white to lighten those sides. Paint the stems with raw umber and shade the left side of each stem with forest green. Paint the cats as desired.

16. Paint the wheelbarrow and fence with heavily thinned hippo grey. Shade the wheelbarrow with very thin charcoal. Smudge very thin streaks of white and charcoal on all parts of the fence. Brighten the right side and the top of the post with a thin coat of white. Shadow the left side of the post and the rails with a very thin coat of charcoal.

Antiquing and Sealing

Mix a small amount of burnt umber oil paint, such as Winton brand, with a solvent-based paint thinner, such as mineral spirits, to create an antiquing stain. Apply a liberal coat of the mixture to the carving. Scrub a small amount of the unthinned oil paint on the outside edge to start the halo. Use a good cotton rag to blend away any hard stain lines, and wipe off the excess. Solvent rags should be dried and disposed of according to the manufacturer's instructions. Paint the rounded edge of the board with full-strength dark burnt umber acrylic paint. Let the acrylic paint dry for 10 minutes, sand it lightly, and apply a second coat.

Allow the stain to dry for a few days. Then, follow the manufacturer's instructions and apply two or three coats of clear satin wipe-on polyurethane to the cleaned back of the carving. Apply four to six coats of the finish to the front and painted edge. After the second coat, and every subsequent coat, buff the finish with a white polishing pad and a piece of crumpled brown paper bag.

Noah's Ark Relief Scene

BY LORI DICKIE

Most folks know the story of Noah: a man was told by God to build an ark and gather two of every species of animal to live with him and his family until the Great Flood was over. This is my interpretation of what Noah and his animal friends may have looked like.

The nice thing about using an egg for this project is that you can use a knife for the whole carving because the shape is rounded. If the wood is flat or square, you often need to use chisels and gouges. For this piece, I carved the front half of the egg in relief and painted the back half with a solid color because it doesn't show. You can use a variety of basswood eggs for this carving; I prefer a goose-size egg. You can buy one with a pedestal attached or purchase the pedestal separately and attach it after you finish the carving.

This carving is fun to make, and is a great gift for a new baby or any fan of Noah's Ark collectibles.

Tools and Materials

- Basswood egg: 2" x 3" (5.1 x 7.6cm)
- Small carving knife
- Woodburner with writing tip
- Black marker
- Pedestal
- Matte varnish finish
- Acrylic paints: beige, black, white, gray, dark yellow
- Water-soluble wax pastels: black, brown, ochre, sky blue, turquoise, ultramarine, violet, white, yellow
- Paintbrushes
- Graphite paper
- Wax-covered paper plate

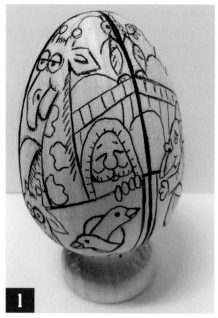

1. Transfer the pattern to the egg. Draw a line down the center of the egg where the grain is straight. This will be the front of the carving. Rotate the egg 90 degrees and draw another line around the egg. Transfer the pattern to the front half of the egg using graphite paper.

2. Make a stop cut along the line that divides the egg in half. Use a carving knife. This separates the carved area from the solid back. Then, make stop cuts around the other figures and elements.

Patterns on
page 93.

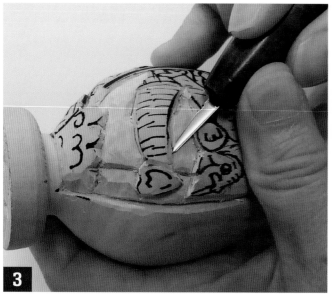

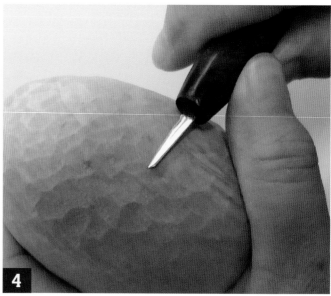

3. Carve up to the stop cuts. Use the carving knife. Begin to carve around the shapes, carving deeper when something is behind another item. Then, make stop cuts and carve the details on the faces, clouds, boat, and water.

4. Add texture to the back and pedestal. Use the knife to remove any machine tool marks and sanded surfaces. You could also leave it smooth and sanded.

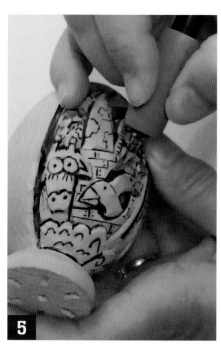

5. Burn all of the details. Use a woodburner. Add the facial expressions and details in the ark and background.

6. Mix acrylic paint with water to create a wash. To darken colors, apply additional thin coats to build up layers of color without hiding the woodburned detail. I like to use the water-soluble wax pastels because they are the perfect consistency for painting over woodburned details. Scribble onto a wax-covered paper plate and add water. Mix with a paintbrush to create a puddle of paint. Apply to the carving like you would acrylic paints.

Painting Guide

- Black
- White
- Gray (elephant trunk)
- Dark yellow (bird beaks)
- Beige (Noah, monkey faces)
- Brown (boat and giraffe spots)
- Ochre (giraffes)
- Violet mixed with white and black (clouds)
- Turquoise mixed with sky blue and white (water)
- Ultramarine (house)
- Yellow (sun)

Noah's Ark Patterns

Centerline

Traditional Ornament

BY GLENN STEWART

My prime carving season starts in the fall and ends around Christmastime. Every year, I carve Christmas ornaments that have a flat back, so they can be worn as a pin. My wife, Judy, enjoys wearing different pins each day during the Christmas season.

Getting Started

Transfer the pattern to the blank. Drill a blade-entry hole and cut the area between the top of the bulb and the ribbon and greenery with a scroll saw or coping saw. Cut the perimeter of the project. Draw a centerline around the edges of the blank.

Tools and Materials

- Basswood, ½" (13mm) thick: 3⅛" x 3⅛" (7.9 x 7.9cm)
- Carving knife
- Detail knife
- Micro gouge: ⅛" (3mm)
- Micro V-tool: ¹⁄₁₆" (2mm)
- Eye punch: ⅛" (3mm)
- Compass
- Needle-nose pliers: small
- Drill with bit: ¹⁄₃₂" (1mm)-dia.
- Woodburner with tips: writing, skew
- Pencil or black marker
- Sanding pads: medium, fine
- Acrylic paints: green, Christmas red
- Paintbrush
- Shoe polish, such as Meltonian shoe cream: #1 neutral, #129 chamois
- Shoe brush
- Cyanoacrylate (CA) glue
- Small paper clip or wire
- Pin back or fine wire
- Toothpick
- Scroll saw or coping saw
- Two-part epoxy

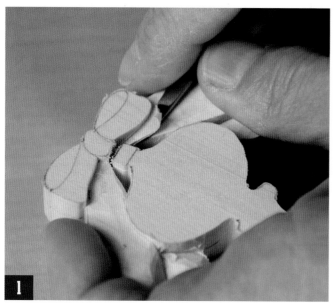

1. Rough out the greenery. Use a detail knife to make stop cuts around the edges of the ribbon and along the sides of the bulb. Use a carving knife to carve the greenery down ⅛" (3mm). Make stop cuts around the lower left greenery, and carve it down an additional ⅛" (3mm).

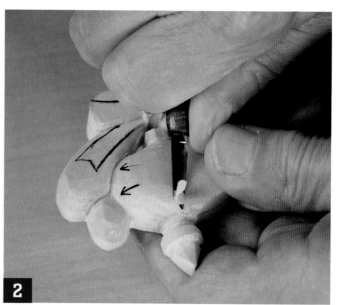

2. Rough out the ribbon and ornament. Redraw the ribbon streamers, and make stop cuts around the streamers and the lower left greenery. Carve away another ⅛" (3mm) from the lower left greenery. Round the bulb from the center to the edges. Carve the top and bottom of the bulb down to ⅜" (10mm) thick. Rough in the top of the bulb.

Patterns on
page 142.

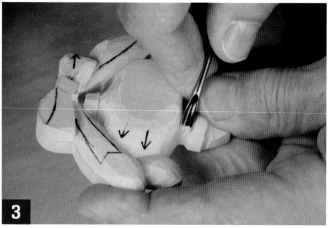

3. Shape the bulb and ribbon loops. Use a ⅛" (3mm) micro gouge to carve the grooves in the bottom of the bulb. The grooves should be about ⅜" (10mm) wide, and the wood at the bottom of the grooves should be ¼" (6mm) thick. Carve the loops on both sides of the knot down ⅛" (3mm). Round the sides of the bulb and ribbon to the centerline.

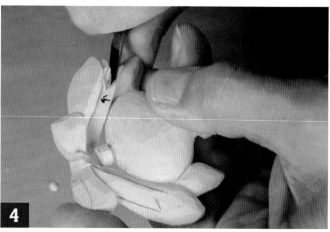

4. Refine the ribbon streamers. Clean up the stop cuts around the streamers. Some of the right streamer is behind the greenery, so taper it with the carving knife. The left streamer is on top of the greenery, so make stop cuts around it and remove wood from the greenery until the ribbon sits on top of the greenery.

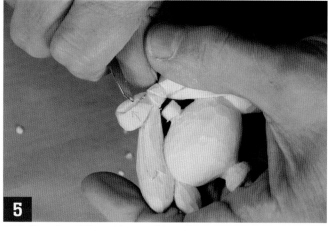

5. Refine the ribbon. Use a ⅟₁₆" (2mm) micro V-tool to add the diagonal groove in the knot. Use the detail knife to make stop cuts in the ribbon loops, and use the carving knife to carve the backs of the loops down to the centerline on the edge of the blank. Refine the back of the bulb to give it more of a 3D effect. Taper the tops of the loops almost to the centerline to make the ribbons look thin.

6. Texture the greenery and top of the bulb. Make short random cuts in the front and back of the greenery with the ⅟₁₆" (2mm) micro V-tool. Do not carve into the ribbon or bulb. Use the micro V-tool to carve the grooves around the top of the bulb. Use the ⅛" (3mm) micro gouge to hollow the top of the bulb. Sand the bulb with a medium-grit sanding pad cut into strips. Then, sand it with a fine-grit sanding pad.

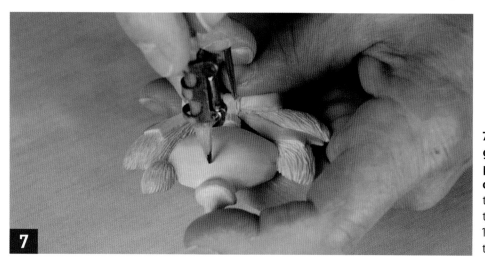

7. Place the point of a compass in the groove in the knot positioned so the pencil will mark both sides of the ornament evenly. Press the point into the knot. Mark a line ¾" (1.9cm) from the point, 1" (2.5cm) from the point, and 1½" (3.8cm) from the point. Carve along the lines with a ⅟₁₆" (2mm) micro V-tool.

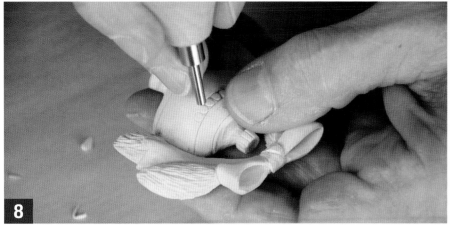

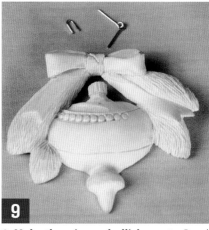

8. Embellish the ornament. Place the edge of a ⅛" (3mm) eye punch in the center of the second V-groove in the center of the ornament. Press it in to make a light circle. Place another circle close to the first one. Continue the circles across the front of the ornament. Use the detail knife to remove the small inverted pyramids between the circles. Deepen the circles with the punch. Then, use the ⅛" (3mm) micro gouge to carve a groove between the top two V-grooves.

9. Make the wire embellishments. Bend a piece of a small paper clip into a *U* shape with needle-nose pliers. Then, create small loops in the end of two additional pieces of another paper clip, and hook the loops together.

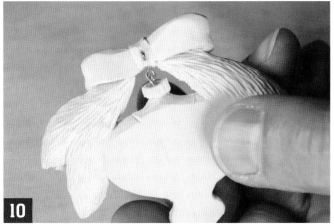

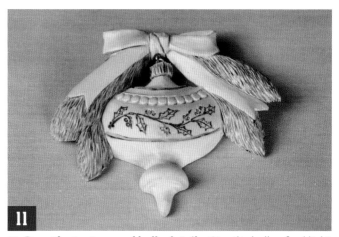

10. Attach the wire embellishments. Drill ¹⁄₃₂" (1mm)-diameter holes for the wires. Drill at an angle into the top of the bulb and the bottom of the ribbon to get the holes in the middle of the blank. The holes don't need to be deep; they just need to hold the wire in place with a bit of cyanoacrylate (CA) glue. Bend the wires parallel with the surface of the ornament. If you plan to use the carving on a tree, add a U-shaped piece of wire for the hanging ribbon.

11. Burn the texture and holly details. Give the bulb a final light sanding where the holly goes. Draw the holly leaves and berries. I use a woodburner with a skew tip to burn the greenery and a writing tip to burn the holly.

12. Paint the ornament. I use thinned Christmas red and green acrylic paint. Apply layers of color to keep the paint from looking thick. For the holly berries, dip a toothpick point in full-strength paint and touch the berries. Allow the paint to dry, and then apply Meltonian shoe cream #129 chamois to the whole carving. Allow it to dry for a few minutes, and then buff it with a shoe brush to bring out some luster. Repeat the process with Meltonian shoe cream #1 neutral. To make an ornament, feed a wire through the top loop. To make a pin, attach a pin back with epoxy.

Whimsical Bank

BY BILL L. POWELL

If you want to carve something whimsical but don't want to deal with cottonwood bark, this project is for you. The beauty of this building lies in the rich details of the logs, bricks, and shingles—and you can add any number of other architectural or framing details. I made a bank, complete with a locking post office box door, but you could easily modify the design to make a birdhouse or a village of buildings by designing a back side and omitting the box door. Much of the carving is done as shallow relief carving, making the pieces easier to handle before assembling them into the larger house.

Getting Started

Cut the pieces to size; I use a table saw. The roof pitch is a simple 45-degree slope, and the tops of the side walls have a matching 45-degree slope. You'll do most of the carving with shallow (#2 or #3) palm gouges. You will find it easier to carve the areas if you have a variety of sizes. The sizes and sweeps I used are in the tool list, but your tools don't have to match exactly to work. Finally, I recommend using a detail knife with a thin blade profile to get the narrow brick joints and shingle separation.

> **Tools and Materials**
> - Basswood, ⅜" (10mm) thick: base, 7" x 7½" (17.8 x 19.1cm)
> - Basswood, ½" (13mm) thick: roof, 6½" x 11" (16.5 x 27.9cm)
> - Basswood, ⅝" (16mm) thick: front and back, 5" x 16" (12.7 x 40.6cm); sides, 5 ½" x 10 ½" (14 x 26.7cm)
> - Post office box door
> - Detail knife: 1¼" to 1½" (32 to 38mm) long thin-profile blade
> - #2 palm gouge: ¾" (19mm)
> - #3 palm gouges: ¼" (6mm), ½" (13mm)
> - #9 or #11 gouge: ³⁄₁₆" (5mm)
> - Micro V-tool: ¹⁄₁₆" (2mm)
> - Scroll saw or coping saw
> - Hammer
> - Nail set
> - Drill press with bits: ⅛" (3mm); Forstner sized slightly larger than window
> - Acrylic paints: arbor green, barn red, camouflage, dark brown, espresso, fawn, gray; vintage white
> - Wiping stain
> - Mineral spirits (to thin stain)
> - Sealer: polyurethane spray
> - Rags
> - Clear acrylic, ⅛" (3mm) thick: sized to fit windows
> - Finishing nails, 1" (25mm) long: 12 each
> - Table saw
> - Wood glue

Instructions

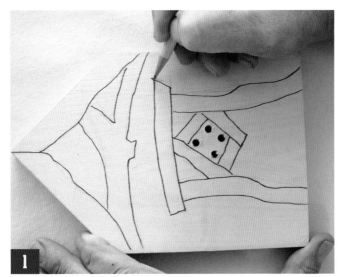

1. Draw or transfer the major design elements to the wood. Drill ⅛" (3mm)-diameter holes through the outer corners of each window. On the back (inside) of each window, drill a ³⁄₁₆" (5mm)-deep hole with a Forstner bit that is slightly larger than the window opening.

2. Cut the window openings. Use a scroll saw or coping saw. Use the detail knife to make deep stop cuts along all the logs and the roofline. You may need to deepen the stop cuts as you remove the wood starting in Step 3.

Patterns on pages 142–43.

155

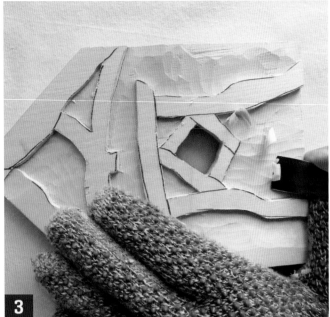

3. Remove the wood from the wall surfaces. Use a ¾" (19mm) #2 palm gouge. Remove about ⅛" (3mm) of wood from around the branches and roofline to create the surface of the plaster. Keep the plaster surface fairly smooth. *Note: Don't remove wood from the outer edges of the front and back until you have glued the pieces together.*

4. Complete the gable shakes, log, door, and doorframe on the front and back. Round the logs with the ¾" (19mm) #2 gouge, making long carving strokes. The gables are just vertical shingles. Make the bottom edges uneven, and separate them with narrow shadow lines (To get realistic shakes and wood for the door, see Three Tips for Dynamic Architectural Details, page 102). Complete the door and doorframe.

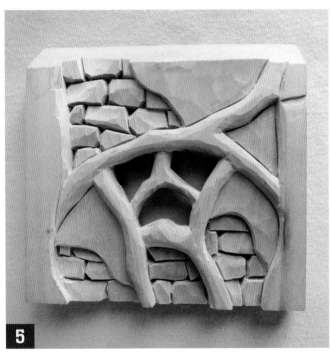

5. Carve the right and left sides. Use the techniques explained in Steps 3 and 4, but do not round the corner logs. The technique to carve bricks is explained in Step 7.

6. Glue and clamp the pieces together. Use wood glue. Make sure the roof angle on the front and back matches the angle cut on the top of the sides. Let the glue dry overnight. Do not use nails or other fasteners in the glue areas because there is more carving to be done on the corners.

7. Make a stop cut where the plaster gives way to bare bricks. Carve down the brick area 1/16" (2mm). Draw the brick pattern. Use the tip of the detail knife to make two angled cuts that meet close to the brick line to create a narrow V-shape. Deepen the joint line as necessary and vary the width of the V-shaped cut. Make shallow facets on the brick faces with a 1/4" (6mm) #3 gouge. Each brick should look different.

9. Clean up the cuts. Use the tip of the detail knife to clean up the fuzzies in the joint lines, log edges, and plaster edges. Carve a three-corner chip in the corner of some bricks to give them a worn look. Add shadow lines along the sides of all the logs by making shallow, narrow V-shaped cuts with a detail knife. Add bark to the logs by making lots of grooves with a 1/16" (2mm) micro V-tool. These grooves should vary in length, depth, and width, and should not be straight.

8. Round the four corner log columns. Use the 3/4" (19mm) #2 gouge. In some places, the logs for the gable extend into the corner logs; mark these areas and carve them first. Make the corners look like logs by removing extra wood in some areas and just rounding other places. Vary the width and thickness of each.

10. Test the fit of the door. If it won't slide easily into the opening, pare down the edges of the door opening or cut some slots where the door mounting tabs meet the jamb. Make sure the door does not hang below the bottom of the opening, or it will not fit after you mount the sides on the base.

11. Trace the outline of the bank onto the base. Draw flagstone walkways in front of the front and back doors. Carve shallow grooves with a ³⁄₁₆" (5mm) #9 or #11 palm gouge to represent the joint lines between the flagstones. Use a ½" (13mm) #3 gouge to remove some of the surface wood on the stones to give them character. Randomly scallop the base edges with a detail knife to remove the saw marks. Take a shallow gouge to all the wood outside the bank walls to remove the machined look.

12. Draw the shingle pattern on the roof pieces. Draw the same number of rows of shingles and make the shingles the same size on both pieces. Use a detail knife to stop-cut along the bottom edge of each shingle. Then, make a narrow V-shaped cut on the sides between each shingle. With a shallow gouge, carve from the base of one shingle to base of the shingle above it. Tip the shingle bottom in random directions and make the lengths vary. Refer to the sidebar for information about the shingle details. Finally, cut matching ¹⁄₁₆" (2mm)-wide by 2" (5.1cm)-long grooves in the roof peaks for the money slot.

Three Tips for Dynamic Architectural Details

1. Avoid using a V-tool. It leaves wide joint lines and comparatively shallow cuts. Instead, make a nearly vertical cut along the joint line with a thin, sharp detail knife, tipping the knife slightly to the left and right to remove a thin sliver of wood much like a chip carving. If necessary, repeat the cut to deepen it and to vary the width of the V-shaped groove along the cut. Do this along the sides of every board, shingle, or brick.

2. Carve each feature individually. That means each shingle or brick has its own face elevation, tip and tilt, and starting and stopping point. Each wood shingle should be a different length and thicker or thinner than its neighbor. Where two boards join or bricks meet, make sure they are not the same thickness where they touch a neighbor.

3. Add shadow lines to every side of every feature. Cut small three-corner triangles at the tips of shingles, ends of boards, corners of bricks, etc. Where siding boards meet trim boards, make a thin, shallow cut alongside the board. At the ends of boards, make a shallow cut where it joins the rest of the carving. With whimsical carvings, the building materials are distressed, so it's hard to do too much corner clipping and outlining.

Painting and Sealing

Paint the bank, base, and roof sections separately. I don't seal the wood before painting. Thin acrylic paints with equal parts water. This thicker mixture produces bold colors. Begin painting with the lightest colors first and progress to darker colors. That way, you can cover any color overrun with a darker paint. When the acrylic paint is thoroughly dry, spray a coat of clear sealer on the surfaces. Thin a dark stain mixed with equal parts mineral spirits. Apply the thinned stain to one side at a time. Quickly wipe off the stain with a rag, leaving it only in the deeper recesses of the carving details. Repeat this on all of the pieces, and buff them with a clean rag to get an aged look.

Assembling

Cut a piece of ⅛" (3mm)-thick clear acrylic plastic the same size as the Forstner bit used to make the window holes. Glue the acrylic into the holes using any suitable glue (there is no strength issue with holding them in).

Drill pilot holes for finishing nails up through the base into the four corner posts. Then, drive nails through the base into the bottom of the corner posts. For the roof, drill four pilot holes in each roof section where it meets the gable. Drive finishing nails into the bank. Use a finishing nail set to drive the head of the nails just below the wood surface, and put a small drop of paint into the depression left by the nail set.

Mount the bank door. If the opening is properly sized, slide the door into the opening and secure it with four screws. Trim as needed with a detail knife to make the door slide in properly.

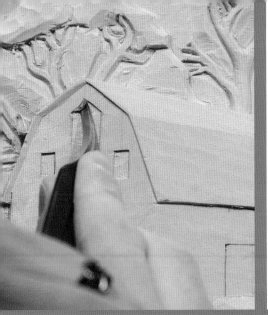

Advanced Projects

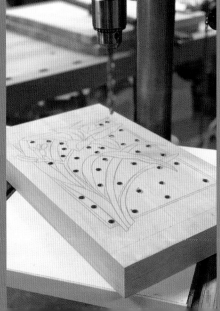

Oak Leaf Frame

BY MARK IVAN FORTUNE

I love miniature decorative frames; they are a functional, fun way to display photos while allowing for creative embellishment. I generally choose wood with a flat, even grain—such as mahogany or lime (basswood)—for carving detailed pieces.

On the other hand, you could try a highly figured wood; it can be risky, but if all goes well, the result can be rewarding. The challenges in this highly figured yew are alternating grain direction and potentially distracting lines, which draw the eye to the grain rather than the carving design. To counteract this, I used deep cuts to lead the eye around the inner oval form. Refer often to the image of the finished piece, noting how the leaves and branches are stacked upon one another, meeting at the top. The more you strategize before you set in, the easier it will be to make decisive cuts.

Getting Started

Align the pattern with the wood grain to best suit the elements of the carving. Attach the pattern to the surfaces of the frame blank and backing plate with spray adhesive. Cut out the backing plate only; I used a scroll saw.

Tools and Materials

- Wood, such as yew, ½" (1.3cm) thick: frame, 5" x 6¾" (12.7 x 17.2cm)
- Basswood, ¹⁄₁₆" (2mm) thick: backing plate, 3" x 4" (7.6 x 10.2cm)
- MDF, ¼" (6mm) thick: 1' x 2' (30.5 x 61cm)
- White paper: sized for MDF backing panel
- Detail knife
- Marking gauge
- #4 gouges: ¼" (6mm), ⁷⁄₁₆" (11mm), ¾" (19mm)
- #6 gouge: ⅛" (3mm)
- #8 gouge: ¼" (6mm)
- #10 gouge: ¹⁄₁₆" (2mm)
- #11 veiner: ⅛" (3mm)
- V-tool: ⁷⁄₁₆" (11mm) 60-degree
- V-tool: ½" (13mm) 90-degree
- Scroll saw with blades: #3 or #5 skip-tooth
- Fret saw (optional)
- Router with bit: straight bit
- Drill with bits: assorted small
- Clamps
- Paint scraper or metal spatula
- Finish: raw linseed oil
- Cloth rags
- Beeswax
- Wood glue
- Spray adhesive
- Toothbrush
- D-ring hook or brace
- Colored pencil
- Sticky tack
- Marking knife

Instructions

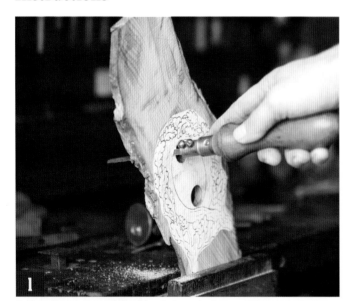

1. Cut the center of the blank. I used a fret saw, but you can use a scroll saw, if desired. Leave the frame within the board for the time being; this will help you hold the work during the preparatory stages—especially when routing the back of the frame.

2. Carefully align the backing board. You can use sticky tack or something similar to steady the assembly.

Patterns on
page 144.

4. Mark the depth of the recess. Use a marking gauge. Use a router and straight bit to cut a ⅟₁₆" (2mm)-deep groove to accommodate the backing plate. I use a router plane. If you do not have access to a router, you can achieve the same result with a V-tool and knife—it will just take longer. Ensure that the backing plate fits snugly, and then set it aside.

3. Trace around the backing with a marking knife. This will score the back of the frame. Hold the backing firmly in place while cutting. To prevent the knife's tendency to follow the grain, make a shallow first pass, getting progressively deeper.

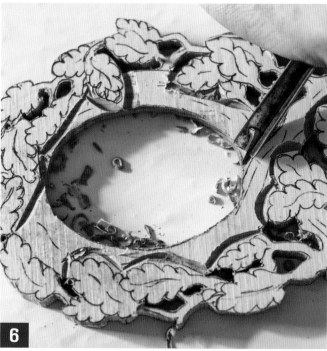

6. Glue the blank to a small stack of white paper (several sheets glued together) secured to an MDF panel. The paper will be easier to dislodge from the back of the finished frame than MDF would. Clamp the panel to your bench. *Note: When gluing your blank to a backing board, make sure the frame back is flush with the backer; gaps may result in breakage when you apply force with an edged tool.* With a ⁷⁄₁₆" (11mm) 60-degree V-tool, part the inner frame from the leaves. Do the same for the overlapping section of the main branch that forms the inner frame.

5. Cut the frame. Drill blade-entry holes for the pierced sections, and then cut them with a scroll saw. Take your time to make smooth, accurate cuts, as this will save unnecessary work in the carving stage. *Note: It helps to mark the waste clearly with a colored pencil to avoid mistakes.*

7. Reduce the height of the inner frame by ¹⁄₁₆" (2mm). Use an inverted ⁷⁄₁₆" (11mm) #4 fishtail gouge, dipping down slightly to form the overlap.

8. Clean up the forms of the leaves. Gently stab the sharp recesses with the ⁷⁄₁₆" (11mm) 60-degree V-tool. Then, refine the curves by stabbing in and releasing the chips; use a ⅛" (3mm) #6 gouge. Finish separating all the forms by making cuts on the sides of the underlying elements. Use a ½" (13mm) 90-degree V-tool.

9. Refine the inner oval of the frame. Round over to the baseline with a ¼" (6mm) #4 gouge.

10. Refine the outer oval of the frame. Use the ⅛" (3mm) #6 gouge.

11. Round the outer leaves. Use an inverted ¾" (19mm) #4 gouge. Taper them down to about ⅛" (3mm) at their thinnest point (farthest from the center).

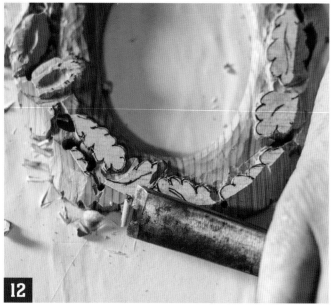

12. Redraw the leaves where necessary. Carve the outline of the leaves with the ¼" (6mm) #4 gouge. Gradually reduce the height of any forms that will be overlapped later.

13. Add life and movement to the leaves and twigs. As you carve the rest of the frame, you will apply the same process to all the leaves and small twigs, giving them slight variation in height. Make two or three cuts across the leaf with a ¼" (6mm) #8 gouge. You can especially accentuate this where you have free space around the leaf, taking full advantage of the thickness of the blank (such as around the edges). Try to visualize the finished leaf as you carve.

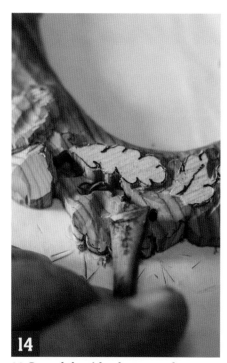

14. Round the ridge between the two previous cuts. Use the ⁷/₁₆" (11mm) #4 fishtail gouge inverted. Apply this technique to all remaining leaves.

15. Draw the central vein. Cut in with a ¹/₁₆" (2mm) #10 gouge. Then, add the veins. Give each lobe a small, curved vein branching from the central one; do this by making gentle stabbing cuts with the ⅛" (3mm) #6 gouge in the direction of growth.

11. Round the outer leaves. Use an inverted ¾" (19mm) #4 gouge. Taper them down to about ⅛" (3mm) at their thinnest point (farthest from the center).

17. Undercut all the leaves. Use the same tool. Stand back from the frame often, continually assessing the sections and severity of the undercuts required. Only undercut what is visually necessary.

18. Texture the main branch. Use a ⅛" (3mm) #11 veiner. With highly figured wood, it may be appropriate to make these cuts quite deep to overcome the eye's tendency to follow the grain, and instead lead it to follow the carved design.

19. Look over the carving. Once you are happy with all elements, carefully separate the carving from the backing with a paint scraper or metal spatula.

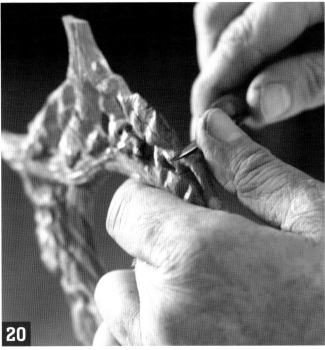

20. Tidy up all the elements. Use a detail knife. Carefully undercut and round the twigs until you are happy with the result.

Finishing

Brush on a thin coat of raw linseed oil. Allow it to soak in for a few minutes before wiping away the excess with a dry cloth. Set aside for a few days to dry. Then, apply a thin coat of beeswax polish with a toothbrush, allowing the finish to harden before buffing with a clean rag. Cut your photo to size secure with backing plate. Add a D-ring hook to hang, or use a brace to hold your frame upright.

Stylized Angel

BY SHAWN CIPA

Gloria in excelsis Deo! Glory to God in the highest! This angel helps capture the true meaning of Christmas and provides a great lesson in relief carving.

This project is a medium-to-deep relief, with an added pierced element, meaning that there is a cutout void. Rather than having a traditional square or rectangular panel, this subject is cut to shape for a more dramatic effect.

Getting Started

Choose a 1" (2.5cm)-thick panel of basswood, free of blemishes, measuring 8" by 16" (20.3 by 40.6cm). Transfer the pattern with your method of choice, making sure that the grain runs vertically. Cut out the shape with a band saw. Drill a blade-entry hole and use a scroll saw or coping saw to make the interior cutout between the left wing and the sphere.

Referring to the pattern, mark the main parts of the piece: the body and banner, sphere, and wings. These parts are defined by surface depth. Use graphite paper and a pencil to draw in other features as the steps progress. Read through all the steps carefully before starting and take your time once you begin. You'll need to secure the piece with clamps during the roughing-out phase; once you get to the details, you may hold it by hand. Strive to smooth all final surfaces as much as possible by leveling the peaks and valleys as you carve; this requires razor-sharp tools, so be sure to strop often.

Tools and Materials

- Basswood, 1" (2.5cm) thick: angel, 8" x 16" (20.3 x 40.6cm)
- Basswood, 1" (2.5cm) thick: stand, 2" x 4" (5.1 x 10.2cm)
- Rough out knife
- Detail knife
- 1" (25mm) hooked skew knife
- #3 gouge: ⅜" (10mm) bent fishtail
- #5 gouges: ⅛" (3mm) detail, ⅜" (10mm) fishtail, 13⁄16" (21mm) fishtail, 13⁄16" (30mm) shallow sweep
- #11 gouge: ⅜" (10mm)
- V-tools: ⅜" (10mm) 60-degree, ⅛" (3mm) 70-degree
- Band, scroll, or coping saw
- Clamps or vise
- Nail punch
- Drill with bit: 3⁄32" (2.5mm)-dia.
- Assorted paintbrushes
- Rubber bands
- Pencil
- Graphite paper
- Blue painter's tape
- Round toothpicks, 4 each 1½" (3.8cm) long
- Wood glue
- Eraser
- Steel wool: 0000
- Wipe-on finish
- White gel stain
- Acrylic paint: gold
- Dyes (optional)
- Cotton cloths
- Colored pencil
- Nail

Instructions

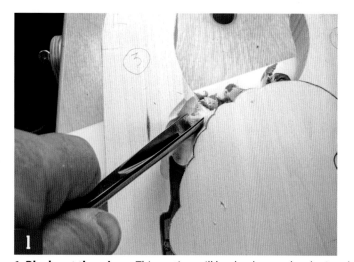 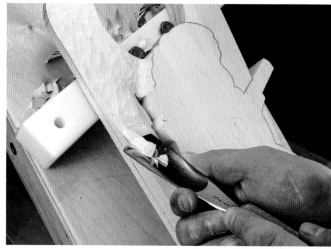

1. Block out the wings. This section will be the deepest level—in other words, the furthest back, and the thinnest. Using a ⅜" (10mm) #11 gouge, create a deep gap where the left wing joins the body. Come as close as you can to the drawn lines, but do not cross them. Set the level by carving to a depth of ⅝" (1.6cm). Then, use a 13⁄16" (30mm) #5 shallow sweep gouge to bring the entire wing to an even thickness of ⅜" (1cm). Use the same technique to block out the right wing, being careful of the lute that crosses over the wing.

Patterns on page 145.

2. Contour the wings. Once you've brought both wings to the proper depth, create a crisp and clean 90-degree wall that follows the contour of the angel. Use the ⅜" (10mm) #11 gouge to scoop out the inner corner, while using a 1" (25mm) hooked skew knife (or another knife of your choice) to clean it up and create the 90-degree angle. Take your time and avoid undercutting during this stage.

4. Shape the banner. Use a ¹³⁄₁₆" (21mm) #5 fishtail gouge to round off the hard corners to achieve a flowing ribbon effect. Make small, shallow chips. Smooth out the void at the very bottom, but keep it separated from the sphere to distinguish it as part of the base.

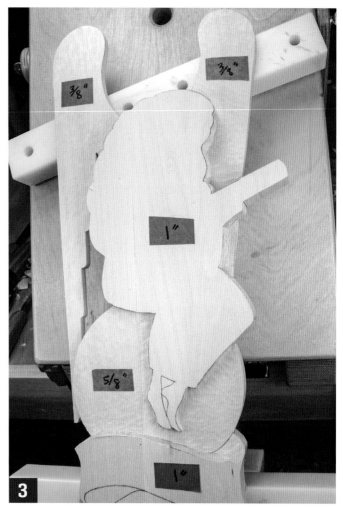

3. Round the sphere. Use the same tools and techniques described in Step 1 and Step 2 to carve the sphere the angel is sitting on to an even depth of ⅜" (1cm). At this point, all initial levels are complete. Label each section with the appropriate thickness; I used pieces of blue painter's tape. Notice that the angel body is untouched, but cleanly outlined by 90-degree angles, and brought forward visually. You'll finish the feet later.

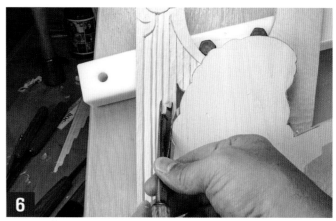

5. Refine the banner. Use a rough out knife to clean up the separations, and then smooth the surfaces as much as possible with the fishtail gouge. Refer to the pattern to pencil in the letters, and then incise them with a detail knife. Then, using the 1" (25mm) hooked skew knife, carefully taper the sphere to create the illusion of a 3D globe.

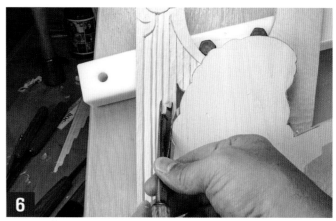

6. Taper the wings. Gradually lower the left wing's thickness until it reaches ³⁄₁₆" (5mm) at the bottom. Mark the wing details with a pencil. Using a ⅜" (10mm) 60-degree V-tool, carefully cut in the lines. Do the same for the right wing.

7. Refine the wings. Round off the hard corners with the rough out knife. Use the same tool to clean up the cuts made by the V-tool. Use a ⅛" (3mm) 70-degree V-tool to further define the feather separations, if desired. Referring to the pattern, mark the main parts of the angel's body, face, hair, sleeves, hands, feet, and lute. You will add detail later.

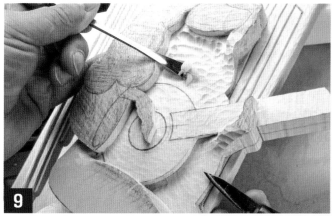

9. Redraw the lute shape. Referring to the pattern, create another lower level by using the rough out knife to plunge cut the walls, while removing material above and below the lute with the ¹³⁄₁₆" (21mm) #5 fishtail gouge. Bring the depth to about ³⁄₁₆" (5mm). Leave extra material around the wrist of the fretting hand, just below the lute's neck, to ensure a smooth transition of the right arm into the sleeve.

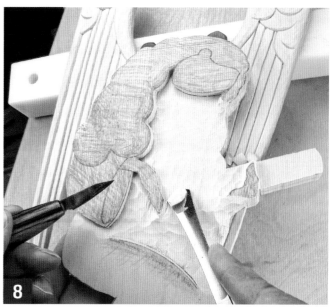

8. Rough out the body. Use a colored pencil to mark the areas that will remain untouched: the face, upper portion of the hair, left sleeve, both hands, and the upper left thigh. Use the rough out knife to stop-cut the perimeter of these areas. Then, use the ¹³⁄₁₆" (21mm) #5 fishtail gouge to remove material from the rest of the body and bring it to an even depth of ¼" (6mm). Level the lowered body area as evenly as possible, especially where the lute's neck will be.

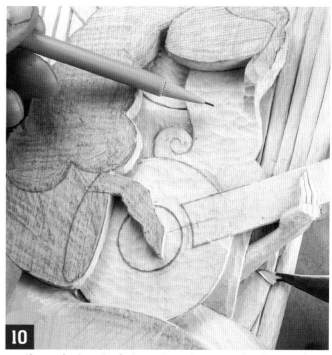

10. Shape the interior hair section. This section has been defined by creating a final ⅛" (3mm)-deep lower level, which serves as the angel's neck and chest area. Use the detail knife to get into the tight areas. Then, use the same tool to carefully carve the left hand. There is little depth to work with here, so take your time to achieve a multiple layered effect: the arm should appear to be emerging from within the sleeve, angled up and outward, while the fingers appear to lay on top of each other, all resting on the lute's neck.

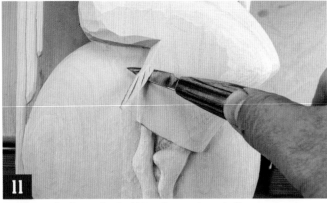

11. Shape the lower body. Using the rough out knife, round and shape the gown. Add a slight separation of the legs in the lap and knees. Round and taper the lower back and body so that the angel appears to be sitting on the sphere. Define the shallow depth of the feet by rounding and removing the two small voids in between. I omitted any toe details here for simplicity, but you can add them, if desired. Smooth the surface as much as possible with the 13⁄16" (21mm) #5 fishtail gouge.

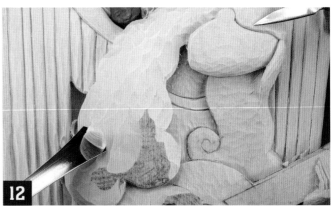

12. Shape the rest of the hair. Using the 13⁄16" (21mm) #5 fishtail gouge, rough out the face and upper hair section by rounding off the hard corners. Use the rough out knife to define an overlapping of the hair above the left sleeve. Define the face details so that the hair appears to hang over the forehead while being tucked behind the ear and jawline. Taper the face in and down toward the chin.

13. Redraw the facial details. Referring to the pattern, pencil in the nose and eyebrows. Using a 3⁄8" (10mm) #3 bent fishtail gouge, gently scallop the higher eye socket area to define the contour of the eyebrow and the bridge of the nose. Use the detail knife to define the nose line and then lower the eyebrow line.

14. Detail the face. Using the detail knife, incise the closed eye slits and lips, and then hollow out the ear. Clean up the cuts, and round the face to its final form. Pencil in the hair curls.

15. Add curls. Using the 1⁄8" (3mm) 70-degree V-tool, trace over the pencil lines to define each curl. Then, use the same tool to create small, scalloped spirals. Use the detail knife to clean up the cuts as you go. Repeat the technique on the inner hair section, as well. Then, use the same tools to detail the sleeve and strumming hand. Add tiny, scalloped cuts to the inside of the sleeve with the 3⁄8" (10mm) #3 bent fishtail gouge.

16. Detail the lute. Use the pencil to mark the star design of the lute's soundhole. Using the detail knife, remove material from the star by making clean, crisp cuts. Add a stippling effect inside the voids by pressing firmly into the surface with a punch; I used a common nail. Then, using the detail knife, incise the separation where the neck joins the body of the lute, and then incise the fret markers.

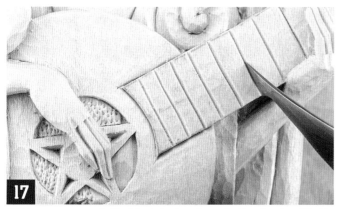

17. Remove material behind the lute's neck. Use the detail knife. Note the curvature of the neck's head. Take your time and proceed carefully while shaping the details; this section is largely cross grain and can easily snap off if you apply too much pressure.

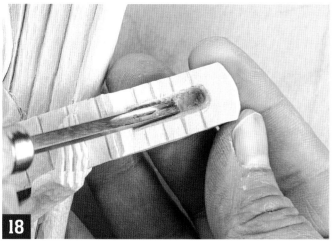

18. Hollow out the lute's head. Referring to the pattern, pencil in the void and add four evenly placed marks to indicate tuning pegs. Using a ⅛" (3mm) #5 shallow detail gouge, carefully hollow out the void to pierce clean through. Use a light touch and support the back with your hand to avoid snapping off the piece.

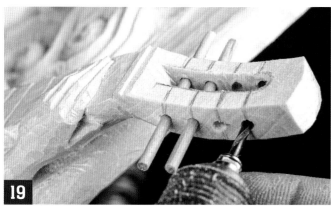

19. Add the tuning pegs. Following the marks, slowly drill holes into one side and out the other with a ³⁄₃₂" (2.5mm)-dia. bit. Ensure that the holes are evenly spaced and parallel to each other. Once complete, insert four 1½" (3.8cm)-long round toothpicks into the holes. If they are loose, apply a small amount of wood glue to the toothpicks. If the fit is tight, glue is not required, as the sealing process will lock them in place. Use an eraser to remove any remaining pencil marks.

Painting and Finishing

Seal the piece with clear wipe-on polyurethane, such as Minwax. Work it thoroughly into all the crevices and deep areas, front and back. Let dry. Lightly sand the entire surface with 0000 steel wool to remove any raised fibers, brush off the debris with a clean cotton cloth, and then apply another coat. Let dry overnight, and then repeat the process for a third and final coat.

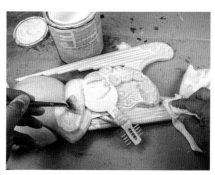

Adding a white gel stain will lighten the overall tone of the wood.

I decided to use minimal color on this piece, but you can add color with dyes or acrylic paints, if desired. Using an artist's fan brush, apply white gel stain, such as Old Masters, to the entire piece. Apply the stain liberally to small sections at a time, working it vigorously into the crevices and deep areas. Quickly wipe off the excess with a clean cotton cloth. Proper application should result in an overall lightening of the wood tone, with heavier staining in the deepest areas, such as the wing overlaps, the hair curls, the inside of the ear, and the area above the banner. Let dry overnight.

Add gold paint. Using an artist's detail brush, apply gold acrylic paint to key areas for a subtle pop of color. I applied it to the robe's collar and hems, the lute, and the tops of the wings. Use an artist's medium flat brush to paint the banner gold, carefully painting around the incised letters so that they remain white. Due to the metallic nature of the paint, several applications may be required to achieve an opaque effect.

Include a base. For a freestanding angel, trace the provided block stand pattern on a piece of scrap. Using wood glue, glue the stand to the back of the carving, flush with the bottom. Use rubber bands to hold it in place until the glue dries. You could also mount the piece to the wall, if desired.

If you'd like your angel to stand freely, glue on a base.

Relief Landscape

BY DYLAN GOODSON

For me, the fun and challenge of working in relief lies in creating the illusion of distance through the depth of the carving. Relief carving has an advantage over carving in the round as you can depict miles of landscape in an inch or two.

For years, I've said that relief carving is working in two and a half dimensions. The finished carving has physical depth, but that depth is not true to life. One inch of depth, for example, might equal 300 miles.

Tools and Materials

- Basswood, 2" (5.1cm) thick: 8½" x 14" (21.6 x 35.6cm)
- #1 chisel: 1/32" (1mm) dogleg (made from a dental pick)
- #2 gouges: ½" (13mm), ¾" (19mm), 1" (25mm)
- #5 gouges: 5/16" (8mm), ½" (13mm), 1" (25mm)
- #7 gouge: 3/8" (10mm)
- #9 gouges: 3/16" (5mm), 11/16" (18mm)
- #11 gouge: 1/8" (3mm)
- V-tools: 1/16" (2mm), 5/16" (8mm)
- Spoon-bent skew chisels: 1/8" (3mm) left, 1/8" (3mm) right
- Woodburner with tips: skew or Guge, micro skew
- Rotary tool with bits: needle-shaped stump cutter, 1/16" (2mm)-dia. cylinder-shaped diamond, 1/32" (1mm)-dia. inverted cone-shaped flute cutter
- Radial bristle discs: 80 grit (yellow), 400 grit (blue)
- Sanding sealer
- Water-based color finish of choice
- Spray satin finish
- Plunge router
- Large flat gouge
- Straight shank tool
- Carving knife

Types of Relief

You can divide relief carvings into three main types: high relief, middle relief, and low relief. Each refers to the amount of depth used to depict the design. In high-relief carvings, the elements protrude 50 to 70 percent of their 3D depth and are extensively undercut. Mount Rushmore is a great example of high relief. Coins, which have barely protruding elements and no undercutting, are examples of low relief. In this landscape, you will be carving in middle relief, which, appropriately, is about halfway between.

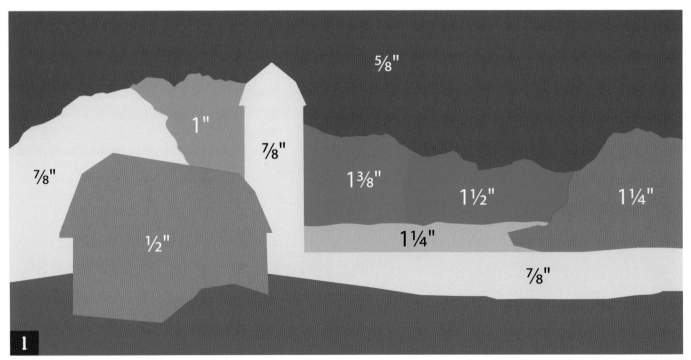

1. Determine the number layers, and where they are to be located. Refer to the levels guide above. I used a plunge router to rough in the levels. Some levels, such as the foreground in this project, taper from one depth to another; I call these levels transition planes. Rough out transition planes to their shallowest depth with the router. You must carve the taper by hand.

Patterns on page 123.

2. Clean up the levels you made with the router. Use a large flat gouge to smooth them. Transfer the final outline of each level to the blank. Make stop cuts on the outlines, using a V-tool or a knife.

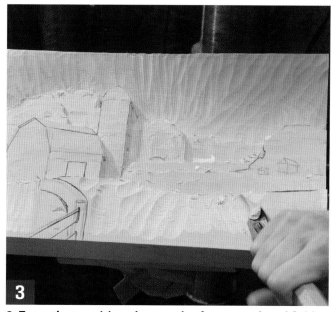

3. Taper the transition planes—sky, foreground, and field— from the shallowest depth to the deepest. Use an 11/16" (18mm) #9 gouge to remove the majority of the wood. Smooth the tool marks with a 1" (25mm) #5 gouge. Deepen the stop cuts (such as around the top of the silo) as needed.

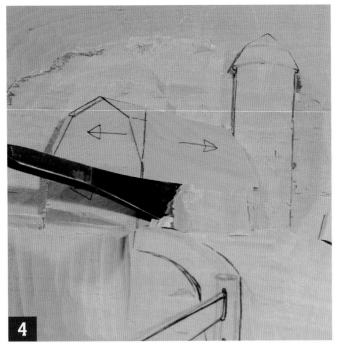

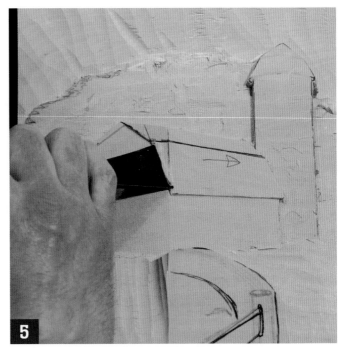

4. Taper the sides and the roof of the barn from the center to the outside corners. Use the 1" (25mm) #2 gouge. Ignore the lines of the roof. Make a stop cut where the barn meets the ground. Leave the outside corners of the barn ⅛" (3mm) above the layer behind the barn. Redraw the roof and eaves lines.

5. Stop-cut the bottom edge of the eaves and the bottoms of the walls. Use a ¹⁄₁₆" (2mm) V-tool. Recess the walls by ¹⁄₁₆" (2mm). Use the 1" (25mm) #2 gouge to carve the planes of the roof. Place the edge of the tool on the line of the rake (the angled edge of the roof), and then carve across the roof following the angle of the wall. Do the plane of the lower section of the roof first and then do the upper section.

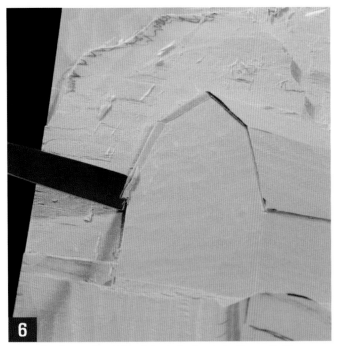

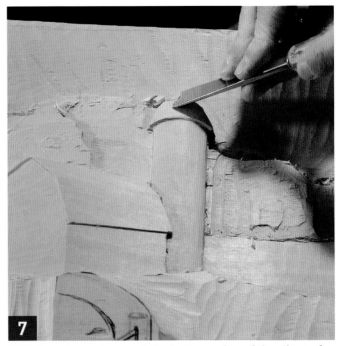

6. Angle the underside of the rake back to the wall. Use a ⁵⁄₁₆" (8mm) #2 gouge. Make sure that the underside of the eave corner wraps behind the wall of the barn.

7. Make a stop cut around the bottom edge of the silo roof. Use the ¹⁄₁₆" (2mm) V-tool. Recess the silo wall by ¹⁄₁₆" (2mm), and round the silo with a ½" (13mm) #2 gouge. Then, round and taper the silo roof.

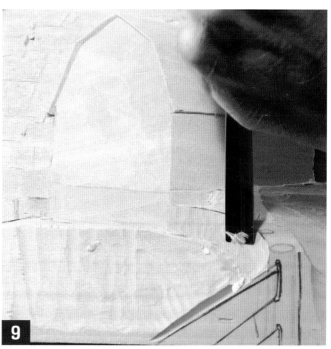

8. Stop-cut around the distant buildings. Then, carve down the trees that are behind the buildings. Shape the buildings using the process in Steps 3 to 6. A set of left and right ⅛" (3mm) spoon-bent skew chisels are helpful, especially around the eaves and gable end of the house, but a straight shank tool will work.

9. Extend the end wall of the barn into the ground to create the barn's exposed foundation. Use the 1" (25mm) #2 gouge to angle the wood for the fence from the top of the nearest fence post to where the top of the fence meets the corner of the barn. Create the vertical plane of the side of the fence with a ½" (13mm) #5 gouge.

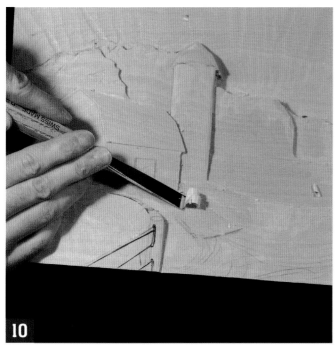

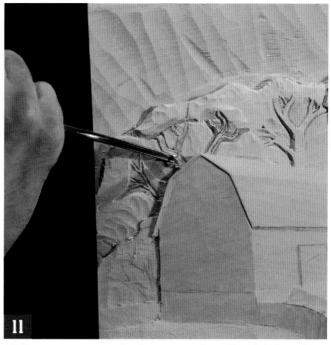

10. Draw the earthen ramp that leads to the side door of the barn. Stop-cut the top and right side of the fence. Slope the near side of the ramp behind the fence. Stop-cut the far side of the ramp to separate it from the ground. Taper the ramp from the side of the barn into the foreground. Use the ½" (13mm) #2 gouge. Blend the ground to the left of the fence to the bottom of the foundation.

11. Recess some areas in the tree sections. Rough in branches and tree trunks in those areas with the 1/16" (2mm) V-tool. Use the knife to refine the shapes of the branches. Round the tops of the trees with a ⅜" (10mm) #7 gouge.

12. Stop-cut around the barn doors and walls. Use a carving knife. Recess the doors with the spoon-bent skew chisels. To make the door look open, stop-cut the center of the door opening, and carve at an angle from the frame to the center. There will be a bit of barn floor showing in the open door.

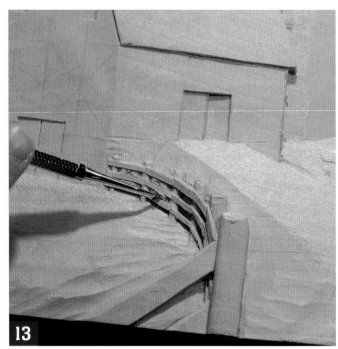

13. Stop-cut around the tops of the fence posts. Remove any extra wood there. Tuck the front of each post behind the fence boards and round the posts. Angle the two fence boards in the foreground behind the nearest post. Recess between them to the depth of the posts. Recess between the fence boards and the posts to the level of whatever is behind the fence. Use the ⅟₁₆" (2mm) V-tool, the spoon-bent skews chisels and a ⅟₃₂" (1mm) chisel.

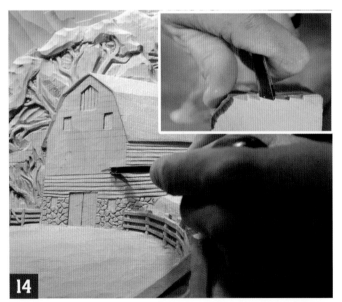

14. Carve the rock texture of the foundation and lap siding. Use the ⅟₁₆" (2mm) V-tool. Create the lapped effect by laying the ⅟₁₆" (2mm) V-tool on its side. Add the vertical boards to the hayloft door by making V-shaped cuts with the knife.

15. Texture the road. Use a ⁵⁄₁₆" (8mm) #5 gouge and a ³⁄₁₆" (5mm) #9 gouge. Make smaller, shallower cuts or use smaller tools as you move towards the background. Texture the far field with the ⅟₁₆" (2mm) V-tool. Space the cuts farther apart as you approach the viewer. Texture the near field with the ⅛" (3mm) #11 gouge. Carve toward the foreground and rotate the gouge onto its side as you carve. That helps taper and fan out the field rows.

Lighting

The interplay of shadows cast by the elements of the carving helps create depth, so try to carve under the same lighting conditions that will be used to display the finished artwork. I have two swing arms mounted on the top of my carving stand that allow me to illuminate the carving from any angle.

16. Burn the metal roof texture on the barn and silo. Use a skew tip or a Guge tip. Use a very low temperature to iron in the ripple texture of the metal; I set my burner to #2 out of 10. Use a higher temperature (#4) to burn the pattern on the silo. Use a micro skew tip at a low heat to detail the window panes, the details of the barn doors, and the distant buildings.

Using Spoon-bent Skews

Small spoon-bent skew chisels have become my favorite tools for small, deep, and tight areas in carvings. You'll need a left and a right angle because, with the bend and angle, they fit into different areas. I use them in three ways:

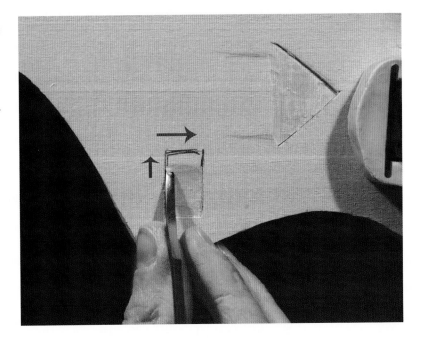

1. **Making regular cuts:** Push the skew straight into the wood like any other carving tool.

2. **Flattening large surfaces:** Push the cutting edge into the wood, and then push the tool sideways. In the photo, I used a left skew and pushed the tool to the right. Repeat this motion, pushing the cutting edge about halfway into fresh wood before starting the sideways slide, letting the heel of the tool rest on the area that was previously cut. Sliding along the previously cut surface will allow you to create a flat, smooth surface even with small tools. Repeat as necessary.

3. **Making stop cuts in tight areas:** Make stop cuts under large overhangs, deep undercuts, or in other tight areas.

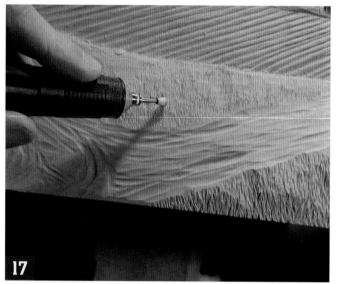

17. Create the grass texture. Use an inverted ceramic cone-shaped bit in a rotary tool. Use a smaller bit for more distant grass. Make the cuts for the closer field as small possible and more uniform than your grass areas. Use a ¹⁄₁₆" (2mm)-diameter ball-shaped diamond bit to stipple the barnyard area, so it looks like dirt trampled by animals.

18. Undercut the barn and silo with the knife. Use the ½" (13mm) #2 gouge to undercut around the top of the silo. Undercut the tree lines with the ⁵⁄₁₆" (8mm) #5 gouge. Where necessary, extend details, like the tree trunks and textures, into the undercuts. Smooth the sky with a ¾" (19mm) #2 gouge.

19. Carve squiggles with a needle-shaped stump cutter to texture the distant tree line. Use a stippling motion with a ¹⁄₁₆" (2mm)-diameter cylinder-shaped diamond bit to texture the trees behind the barn. Use the same technique with a ¹⁄₃₂" (1mm)-diameter inverted cone-fluted cutter to texture the trees around the distant buildings. Vary the primary direction of the texture from one tree to the next to create better depth. Use an 80-grit (yellow) radial bristle disc to de-fuzz all the power carved areas. Remove any remaining pencil marks with a 400-grit (blue) radial bristle disc.

> ## Tip: Cleaning Undercuts
>
> The spoon-bent skews excel at cleaning out the undercuts. Diamond rifflers are a fantastic way to pick or sand away those last few slivers that never want to come out of the undercuts.

Finishing

Stain will bring out all the details of your relief carving, but it makes some varieties of wood blotchy. To prevent this, seal the carving with two coats of sanding sealer. Brush on a coat of a water-based color finish of your choice. Use a rag to wipe off the excess glaze. Then, use the rag and brush to even out the amount of glaze on the carving. Leave the glaze thicker or apply a second coat on areas that you want to be shadowed. After the glaze dries, apply two light coats of clear satin finish. Buff the finish with a crumpled brown paper bag after each coat.

Relief Landscape Pattern

Elegant Floral Relief (Daylily)

BY ROSANNA COYNE

The Daylily (*Hemerocallis*) is a perennial plant whose flowers typically last about a day. Its scientific name is derived from two Greek words: hemera, meaning day, and kallos, meaning beauty. The short-lived nature of the daylily served as my inspiration for this carving. I captured the bloom in relief as a reminder to live in the present moment.

Carving in high relief depicts the subject at approximately three-quarters or more of the original object's thickness. Bringing the form away from the ground requires a high degree of undercutting, giving the piece a sense of definition and creating shadows for added drama. However, in undercutting, one must practice restraint. Too much and you risk weakening the carving and creating areas that can be difficult to clean up.

Tools and Materials

- Basswood or cherry, 1¾" (4.4cm) thick: 9¾" x 16¾" (24.8 x 42.6cm)
- #1 gouges: ¹⁄₃₂" (1mm), ½" (13mm), 1" (25mm)
- #2 gouges: ¹⁄₁₆" (2mm), ³⁄₁₆" (5mm), ⁵⁄₁₆" (8mm), ½" (13mm), ⅝" (16mm)
- #2 spoon gouges, left skew: ³⁄₁₆" (5mm), ⁵⁄₁₆" (8mm)
- #2 spoon gouges, right skew: ³⁄₁₆" (5mm), ⁵⁄₁₆" (8mm)
- #3 gouges: ⅛" (3mm), ⁵⁄₁₆" (8mm), ½" (13mm), ⅝" (16mm) fishtail
- #5 gouges: ³⁄₁₆" (5mm), ⁵⁄₁₆" (8mm) fishtail, ½" (13mm)
- #7 gouge: ³⁄₁₆" (4mm), ⁵⁄₁₆" (8mm) fishtail
- #8 gouges: ¹⁄₁₆" (2mm), ³⁄₁₆" (4mm), ⁹⁄₁₆" (14mm), ¹¹⁄₁₆" (18mm)
- V-tools: ¹⁄₁₆" (2mm) 60-degree, ³⁄₁₆" (5mm) 45-degree long bent, ¼" (6mm) 45-degree
- #28 back bent gouge: ¼" (6mm)
- Hooked skews: ⁹⁄₁₆" (14mm), ¾" (19mm)
- Metal or wood mallet
- Marking gauge
- White buffing pad
- Drill with bits: ⅛" (3mm), ⅜" (10mm)-dia
- Pencil
- Tracing paper
- Tape or pins
- Carbon paper
- Assorted brushes
- Bristle brushes: 2 each White China
- Sandpaper: assorted grits (optional)
- Clean cotton cloths
- Finish
- White burnishing pad
- Drill press with a depth stop

Getting Started

Make a full-size drawing of the design on tracing paper. Mark centerlines through the width and length of the design, and make similar marks on the wood. Always work with centerlines, as this ensures that the design stays centered and square. Tape or pin the drawing to the blank, slip carbon paper underneath, and transfer the design.

Tip: Hand-Drawing Patterns

Resist the temptation to transfer the design with techniques other than hand-drawing (i.e. hot iron transfer or glue). Repetition builds muscle memory, strengthens your fingers, and cements the design in your mind.

Patterns on page 146.

Advanced Projects: Elegant Floral Relief (Daylily) **125**

Instructions

1. Mark the depth. Using a marking gauge, draw a line ¾" (1.9cm) from the bottom around the board for the frame thickness. The surrounding frame will be lowered to allow the daylily to overlap it, standing proud of the frame. Then, establish the depth. Using either a drill press with a depth stop or a hand drill with a ⅜" (10mm)-dia. bit and a stop collar, drill holes in the background areas inside the frame, just shy of the final depth of 1¼" (3.2cm). Leaving some material will give you enough wood to clean up the background. Switch to a ⅛" (3mm)-dia. bit to reach the tight areas.

2. Outline the design. Cut away the wood from the background areas using a 3/16" (5mm) 45-degree V-tool and a mallet. Outline the subject, being sure to stay about 1/16" (2mm) away from the lines.

3. Lower the background. Using a gouge with a deep sweep, such as an 11/16" (18mm) #8, begin to remove the background material, making cuts across the grain. Move to smaller gouges to access the areas between the leaves. As you progress, you will need to pare down the walls to remove material from the background. You will do this in several stages until you reach the scribed line on the sides of the board, which signifies the frame thickness.

4. Refine the lines. Using various sweeps to match the curves of the pattern lines, pare down to the pencil lines, making sure your walls are perpendicular to the surface of the blank. *Note: Try your best not to leave stab marks in the background.* This area will be undercut, and these marks will show later.

5. Smooth the frame area. Use a ⅝" (16mm) #2 gouge. Make organized slicing cuts across the grain, skimming off the ridges. Work down to frame depth. *Note: In order to avoid tear-out on the edges of the board, avoid carving across the grain to the edge, rather starting from the edge and moving inward.* Establish the inside edge of the frame using a marking gauge, and then pare down the background areas within that line using a 1" (25mm) #1 gouge.

6. Continue refining the background. Use narrower gouges, such as a ³⁄₁₆" (5mm) #2 gouge and a ½" (13mm) #2 gouge. Using the short bent ³⁄₁₆" (5mm) #2 spoon gouge (both left and right skews) is helpful in the tight areas between the leaves. Work down to just above the final depth.

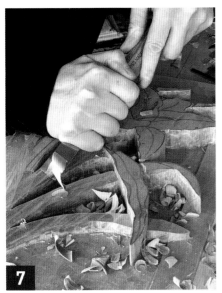

7. Shape the leaves. Separate the forms that cross over each other using the ³⁄₁₆" (5mm) 45-degree V-tool. Mark the high spots, areas where you will not remove wood and from which the form slopes downward, with a pencil. Lower the stem with the ⅝" (16mm) #2 gouge, continuing onto the leaves and finally the flower head. Slope the leaves down to the stem where appropriate, referring to the image of the finished product on page 125 (or photos of actual daylilies). Capture the twists and turns of the leaves while maintaining flow and continuity. Then, where necessary, redraw the lines that were removed during roughing. Define the primary stem with a ¼" (6mm) 45-degree V-tool, being mindful of grain direction. *Note: Do not be tempted to start undercutting at this stage.* If further shaping is needed on an undercut edge, there simply will not be enough material to carve.

8. Rough shape the emerging flower buds and stem. Slope them down toward the frame edge with a ½" (13mm) #5 gouge. Define each bud using the ¼" (6mm) 45-degree V-tool, and shape them into cylinders using ⁵⁄₁₆" (8mm) #3, #5, and #7 fishtail gouges.

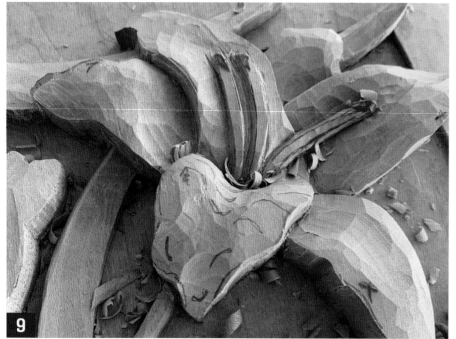

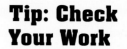

9. Shape the flower head. When doing this, note the various overlaps, as well as the fact that there are no plane surfaces. Each petal is composed of compound curves. Separate the petals using the ¼" (6mm) 45-degree V-tool. Then, rough out the petals with the ½" (13mm) #5 gouge, defining the areas where they overlap. Round the tops of the ridges using the gouge flute-down. Shape the petals so they appear to emerge from the throat of the daylily. Redraw the stamens and clean up their outlines with the ¼" (6mm) 45-degree V-tool.

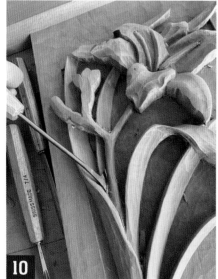

10. Detail the stem and leaves. Start with the leaves closest to the background, adding details, such as the curling of the leaves. Use a ½" (13mm) #5 gouge. Proceed to the next levels and finally the flower head. Working in such an organized way protects the leaves at higher levels from tool damage. Switch to the 9/16" (14mm) hooked skew for the tight areas where the secondary stem meets the leaves.

11. Create the leaf waves. Add an undulating motion to the leaves with a 9/16" (14mm) #8 gouge, carving a channel from the high part of the lobe to the lower part with a twisting motion. Smooth the ridges and round-over the outside edge of the upper lobe with a 5/16" (8mm) #5 fishtail gouge. Add a similar undulating motion to the flower petals. Use the 3/16" (5mm) #5 gouge.

12. Refine the leaves. Give them a convex shape using the ½" (13mm) #5 gouge. It is important that the leaves flow continuously behind one another and the flower head and buds. Smooth with the 5/16" (8mm) #3 fishtail gouge or a tool of your choice. It may be necessary to carve against the grain in certain areas, but skewing the tool with a slicing cut will leave a smooth surface.

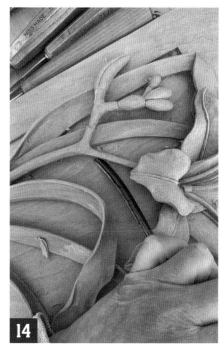

13. Refine the petals and buds. Add veining to the petals using the ¼" (6mm) 45-degree V-tool. First, make two parallel cuts to define the vein. Then, round over the vein with a ¹⁄₁₆" (2mm) #8 gouge and remove the ridges with the ⁵⁄₁₆" (8mm) #5 fishtail gouge.

14. Start undercutting. To add shadow and depth, carve under the edges of the petals and leaves, but not so much that it weakens the object's bond to the background. In undercutting a curved edge, use a gouge whose curve is flatter than the edge itself, and then clear away the chip with a spoon gouge. Neatly undercut the deep recesses and corners using a ³⁄₁₆" (5mm) 45-degree long bent V-tool. Thin and shape the stamens to final width, and then undercut them. Use the same tool.

Finishing

Apply finish; for this project, I chose to go with Osmo Polyx-Oil. I wanted a finish that was easy to use and nontoxic, without an overpowering scent. Made from natural vegetable oils and waxes, this product goes easy on the environment. Apply with a brush to reach the nooks and crannies of the carving, let it penetrate, and then wipe it off with a white burnishing pad and a dry brush. Allow at least 24 hours for the finish to dry. Apply several coats to reach your desired sheen.

15. Smooth the background. Clean up any unfinished spots, making sure the background lies at the same level in all areas. Smooth over all ridges and add finishing touches. Whether you choose to sand your work or give it a tooled finish is up to you. If you elect to sand, move up progressively through the grits to remove tool marks. A tooled finish, on the other hand, requires you to go over the entire piece to remove ragged cuts, softening any sharp edges using an assortment of freshly sharpened gouges. Once done, bevel the edge of the inner frame and the outside with a ⅛" (3mm) chamfer using the ½" (13mm) #2 gouge.

Patterns

Bark Fairy Door Pattern

Project on page 14.

Photocopy at 100%

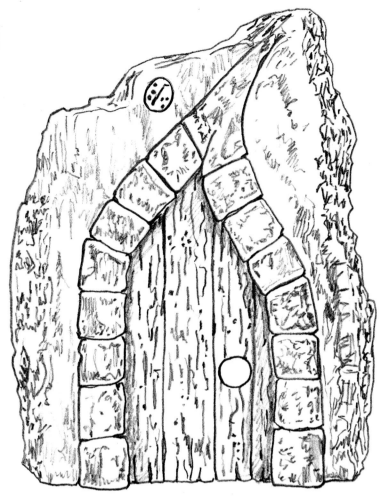

Honeybee Pattern

Project on page 56.

Photocopy at 100%

Flower Garland in Mahogany Pattern

Project on page 62.

Photocopy at 100%

Crescent Moon Pattern

Project on page 18.

Photocopy at 115%

Holiday Star Pattern

Project on page 24.

Photocopy at 100%

⅜"-diameter hole

Twig and Leaf Drawer Handles Patterns

Project on page 28. Photocopy at 100%

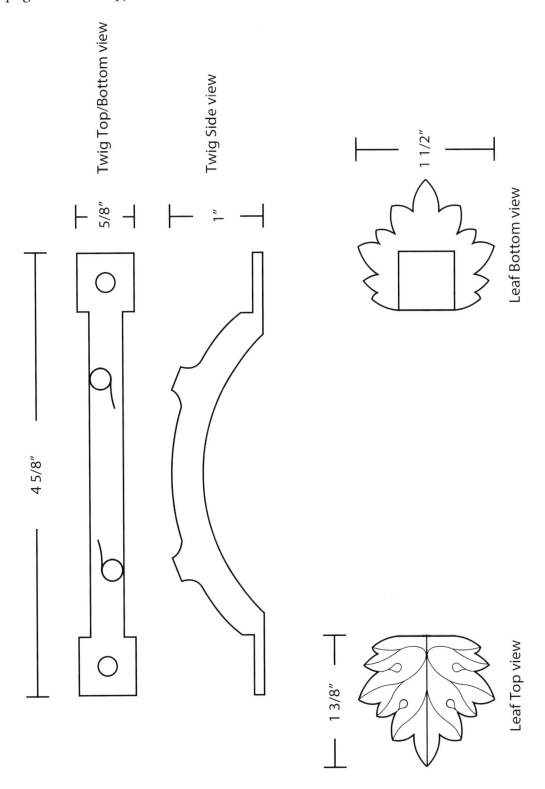

Twig Top/Bottom view

Twig Side view

5/8"

1"

4 5/8"

1 1/2"

Leaf Bottom view

1 3/8"

Leaf Top view

Sailboat Pattern

Project on page 34.

Photocopy at 100%

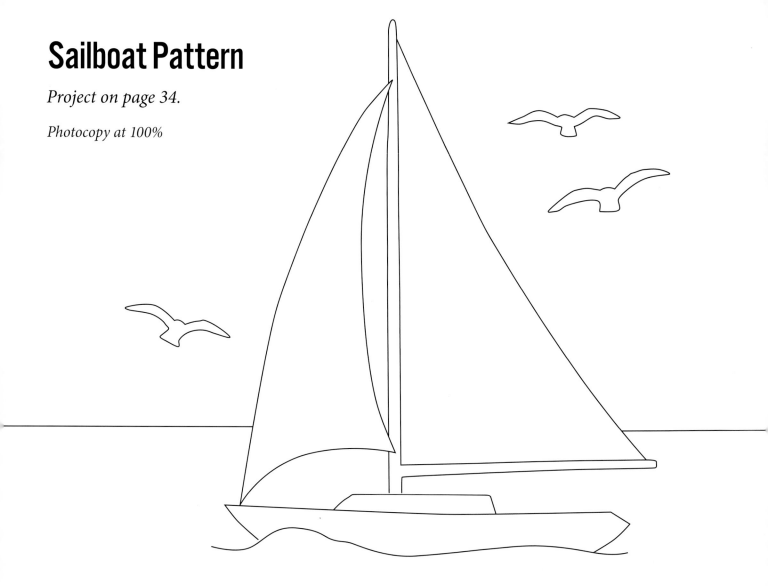

Frank the Sweet Greeter Paint Pattern

Project on page 42. Photocopy at 100%.

Flower Barrette Patterns

Project on page 46.

Photocopy at 100%

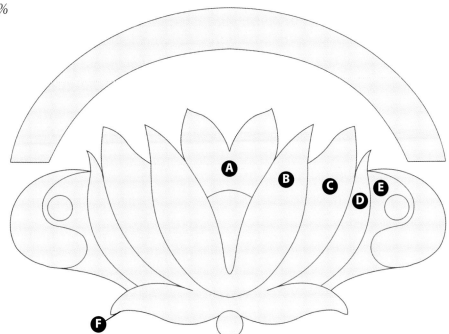

Floating Leaf Pattern

Project on page 38. Photocopy at 100%

Miniature Acanthus Patterns

Project on page 50.

Photocopy at 100%

Rosette Box Patterns

Project on page 66.

Photocopy at 100%

.

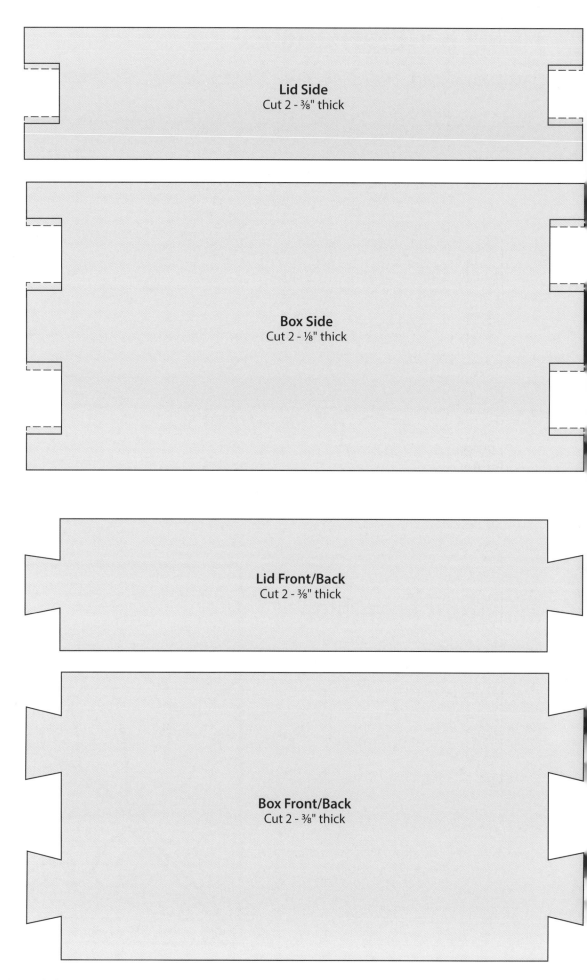

Lid Side
Cut 2 - ⅜" thick

Box Side
Cut 2 - ⅛" thick

Lid Front/Back
Cut 2 - ⅜" thick

Box Front/Back
Cut 2 - ⅜" thick

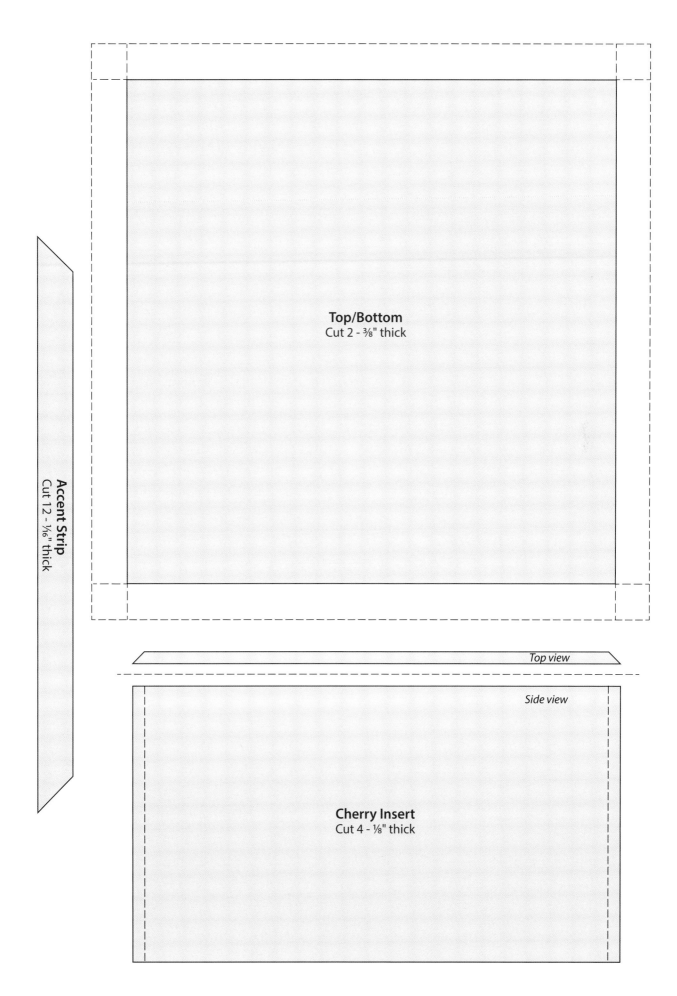

Accent Strip
Cut 12 - ¹⁄₁₆" thick

Top/Bottom
Cut 2 - ³⁄₈" thick

Top view

Side view

Cherry Insert
Cut 4 - ⅛" thick

Rosette
Pattern

Project on page 66.

Photocopy at 100%

Celtic Knotwork Pattern

Project on page 72. Photocopy at 100%

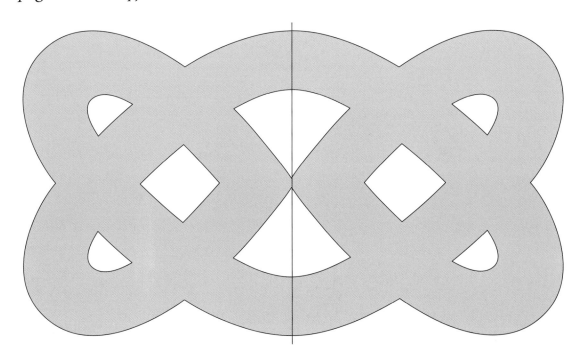

Botanical Woodland Print Pattern

Project on page 76. Photocopy at 100%

Sunken Greenman Pattern

Project on page 81. *Photocopy at 100%*

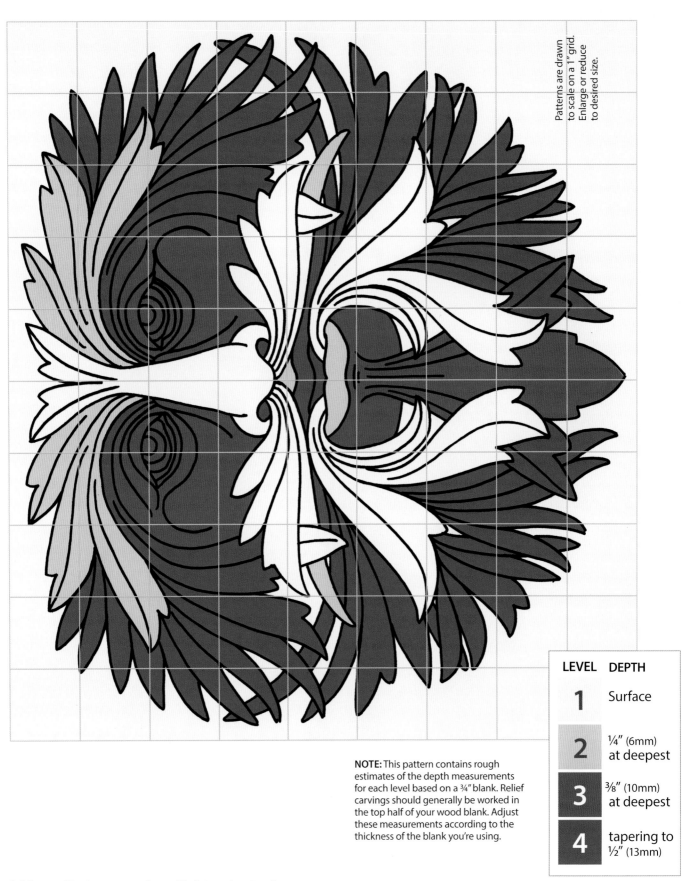

Patterns are drawn to scale on a 1" grid. Enlarge or reduce to desired size.

LEVEL	DEPTH
1	Surface
2	¼" (6mm) at deepest
3	⅜" (10mm) at deepest
4	tapering to ½" (13mm)

NOTE: This pattern contains rough estimates of the depth measurements for each level based on a ¾" blank. Relief carvings should generally be worked in the top half of your wood blank. Adjust these measurements according to the thickness of the blank you're using.

Fall Scene in Low Relief Pattern

Project on page 84.

Photocopy at 150%

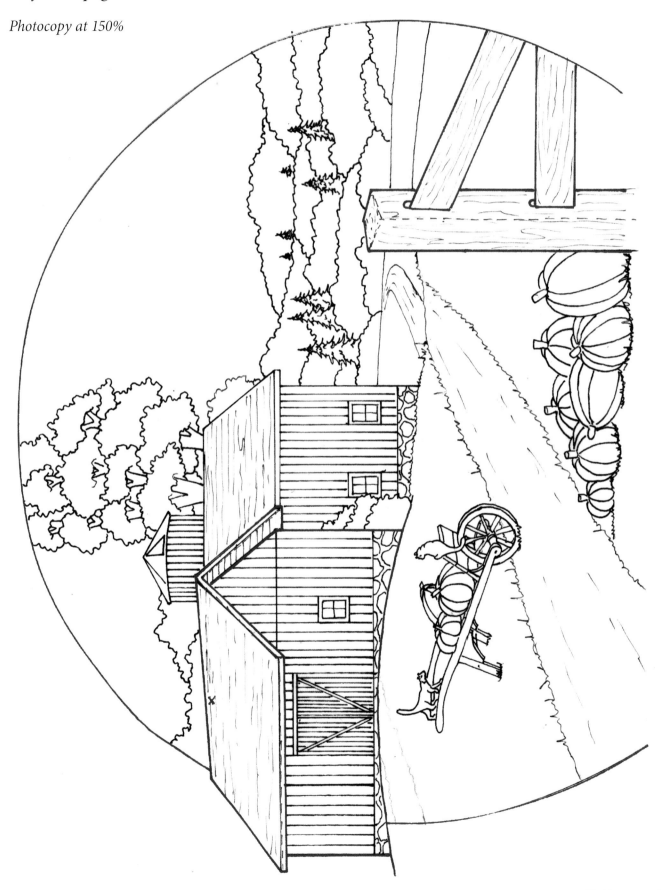

Traditional Ornament Patterns

Project on page 94. Photocopy at 100%

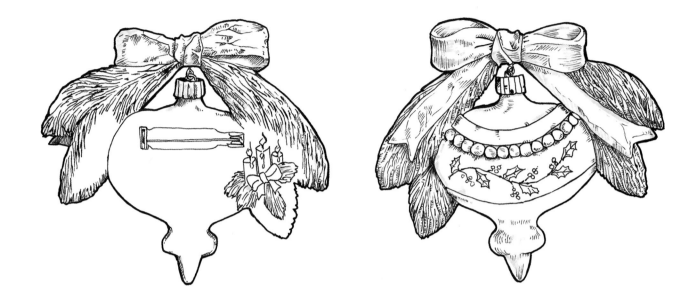

Whimsical Bank Patterns

Project on page 98.

Photocopy at 150%

Each block of this grid equals 1″ in proportion to the original pattern. Enlarge this art to 150% to fit the PO box door.

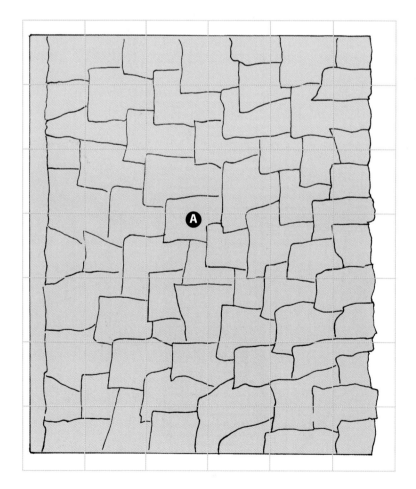

Whimsical Bank Patterns
Project on page 98. Photocopy at 150%

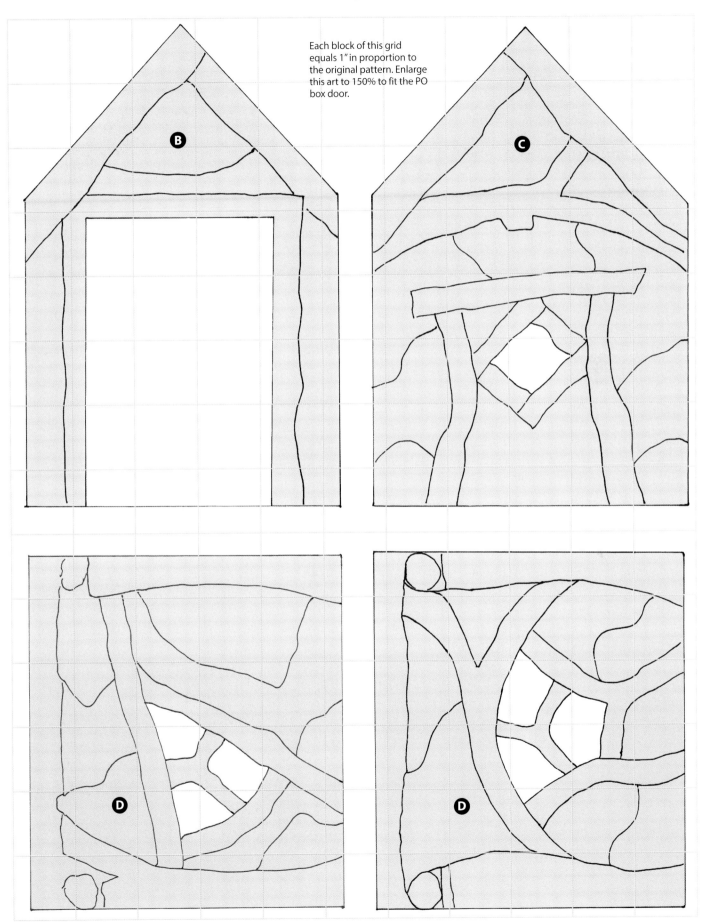

Each block of this grid equals 1" in proportion to the original pattern. Enlarge this art to 150% to fit the PO box door.

Oak Leaf Frame Patterns

Project on page 104.

Photocopy at 100%

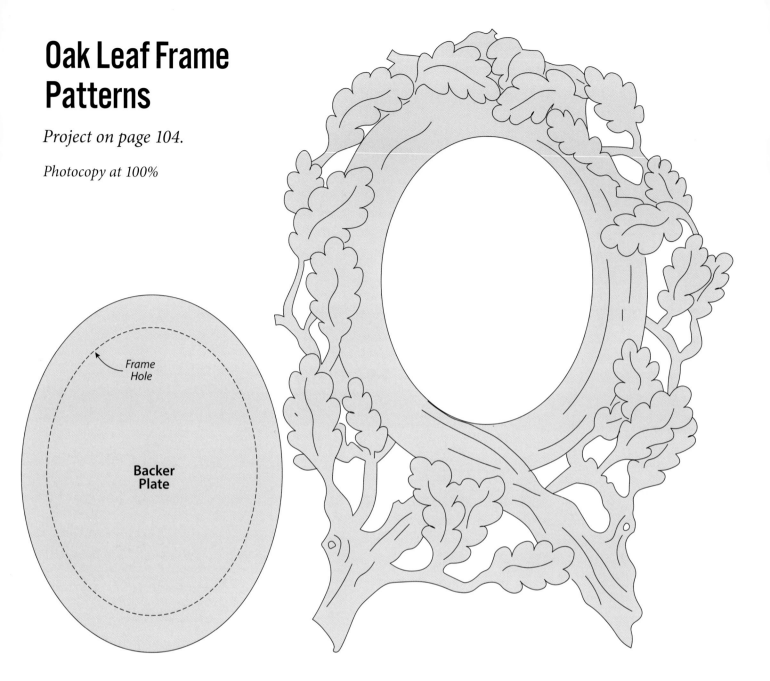

Frame
Hole

Backer
Plate

Stylized Angel Patterns

Project on page 110.

Photocopy at 100%

Elegant Floral Relief (Daylily) Pattern

Project on page 124.

Photocopy at 200%

Index

Page numbers in *italics* indicate projects and **bold** indicates patterns.

J

K

L

M

N

O

P

R

S

T

U

V

W

About the Authors

 **Janet Bolyard** resides in Lakeside, Arizona, where she is enjoying her retirement—which consists of a lot of woodcarving and woodworking.

 **Shawn Cipa** was recognized as "Santa Carver of the Year" after he won Woodcraft's National Santa Carving contest. He is the author of several books with Fox Chapel Publishing. Shawn accepts commissions for his work and can be contacted at *shawncipa.com*.

 **Rosanna Coyne** has been woodcarving professionally since 1997 from her home studio in Hampden, Massachusetts. To see more of Rosanna's work, visit *rosannacoyne.com* and @rosannacoyne on Instagram.

 **Lori Dickie** lives on a small farm in Michigan with her husband, Steve. She has been carving for 20 years and displays her work at local shows. Find her on Etsy at lmdickie1.

 **Richard Embling** lives in Wales, UK. He has been carving since the age of 12 and originally got interested in carving decorative walking sticks and traditional wooden puppets. Over the past few years, his focus has moved to character carving. Working as a lecturer in the creative arts, he has found his passion for teaching translating into his love of woodcarving. Find more examples of his work on his Instagram and Facebook @TheUrbanTinker.

 **Mark Ivan Fortune** followed a traditional apprenticeship in stone carving to become a master of his craft with more than 20 years of experience. Since 2008, he has turned his attentions primarily to woodcarving. He teaches from his home workshop at Raheenwood in East Clare, Ireland.

 **Lucy Fox** lives in Kingston upon Thames in the UK and carves from a workshed at the end of her garden. She has been carving for some years and takes her inspiration from nature and classical woodcarvers whose work can be seen in old churches and museums. While she mainly carves in relief, she has been working more 'in the round' and hopes to improve in this area going forward. Find more of her work on Instagram @lucyfoxcarvings.

 Born and raised in Alabama, **Dylan Goodson** is a recent transplant to Michigan's Upper Peninsula, where he lives with his woodcarving wife, Barb. When not snowed in, he travels the country teaching carving seminars and participating in carving shows and competitions. His website is *www.oldoakenterprises.com*.

 **Ivan Govaerts** is a professional firefighter living in Belgium. As a self-taught artist, he spends his free time in his workshop. He started woodburning as his main activity in 2000, but tries to combine this with woodcarving and woodturning. Get more info about Ivan at *woodcreator.be* or Instagram @macro_woodcreator.

Lora S. Irish is an author, artist, carver, and pattern designer residing in Mount Airy, Maryland. She has written Landscape Pyrography: Techniques and Projects, Crafting with Gourds, Finishing Techniques for Woodcrafters, and many other Fox Chapel Publishing books. For more of her work, visit *lsirish.com*.

Robert Kennedy, of central Arkansas, has been carving a variety of subjects—both in relief and in the round—for 16 years. See more of his work on his Instagram page @rlk_wood_carving.

Lisa Laughy is a professional woodcarver and artist living in central New Hampshire. She is a juried member of the League of New Hampshire Craftsmen and enjoys designing and creating woodcarvings that combine her love of nature with her interest in Celtic art. You can learn more about her work at *ninthwavedesigns.com* or on Instagram at @ninthwavedesigns.

Adria Laycraft is a sci-fi author, book editor, and woodcarver from Calgary, Alberta, Canada. You can watch her carve, bark hunt, and interview other woodcarvers on her YouTube channel, Carving the Cottonwood Adria Laycraft. Learn more at *adrialaycraft.com*.

Beth Lewis is a freelance printmaking artist and designer based in Cornwall, England, where she lives with her husband and 3-year-old daughter. There, they run a woodland event space, and Beth runs an online shop selling woodcut and linocut prints, stationery, and handcarved stamps.

Mary May is a European-trained professional woodcarver specializing in classical and period designs and techniques. She works on furniture and architectural commissions and teaches woodcarving at a variety of schools throughout the United States and Europe. Mary runs Mary May's School of Traditional Woodcarving, an online video school offering hundreds of different lessons for all skill levels. She has appeared several times on Roy Underhill's The Woodwright's Shop and recently completed her first book of over 300 pages, *Carving the Acanthus Leaf*. Find more of Mary's work at *marymaycarving.com*.

D. L. Miller grew up in the Appalachian Mountains of Western Maryland and now resides in Boiling Springs, Pennsylvania. He has a B.A. in fine arts. Today, much of his work is focused on combining techniques and mediums he has learned over the years as a painter, carver, and resin artist, with primary focus on scenes found in nature.

Bill L. Powell is a retired foundry technical director. He carves with the Happy Trails Sawmill Carvers and Cactus Carvers of Surprise Arizona. Bill has been carving for 10 years and likes to carve whimsical bark houses, relief, and Scandinavian flat plane figures.

Glenn Stewart has been carving for more than 30 years. He lives in Hawesville, Kentucky, with his wife, Judy. They have two daughters, two granddaughters, one grandson, and one great-grandson.

Elaine and Fred Stenman live in Wisconsin and winter in the Rio Grande Valley of Texas. They have been selling woodcarvings at art shows for forty years. They have been teaching for over thirty years. Fred is the major design force, while Elaine is more involved in production. See more of their work at *stenmanstudios.com*.

Dustin Strenke is a self-taught woodcarver who has been carving part-time for approximately nine years. He lives in a small town in Northwest Wisconsin and is a full-time patrol deputy with the local sheriff's department. He owns a small business called Chiseled Outdoors Custom Carvings, which focuses primarily on wildlife-themed artwork. Find more of his work on YouTube @ChiseledOutdoorsCC, on Etsy at ChiseledOutdoors, or on Instagram @chiseled_outdoors.